HITLER'S SAVAGE CANARY

HITLER'S
SAVAGE CANARY

A History of the Danish Resistance in World War II

DAVID LAMPE

Foreword by Birger Riis-Jørgensen,
Ambassador of Denmark, London

Frontline Books, London   Arcade Publishing • New York

HITLER'S SAVAGE CANARY: A History of the Danish Resistance in World War II

First edition published in 2010
by Frontline Books, an imprint of Pen & Sword Books Limited,
47 Church Street, Barnsley, S. Yorkshire, S70 2AS
www.frontline-books.com

and

Published and distributed in the United States of America and Canada
by Arcade Publishing, 307 West 36th Street, 11th Floor, New York, NY 10018
www.skyhorsepublishing.com

Arcade Publishing books may be purchased in bulk at special discounts for sales promotion,
corporate gifts, fund-raising, or educational purposes. Special editions can also be created to
specifications. For details, contact the Special Sales Department, Arcade Publishing, 307 West
36th Street, 11th Floor, New York, NY 10018 or arcade@skyhorsepublishing.com.

Arcade Publishing® is a registered trademark of Skyhorse Publishing, Inc.®, a Delaware
corporation.

ISBN 978-1-62872-371-7

PUBLISHING HISTORY
The Savage Canary: The Story of Resistance in Denmark was first published by Cassell &
Company Ltd London in 1957. This edition contains a revised plate section and a new foreword
by Birger Riis-Jørgensen, Ambassador at the Embassy of Denmark in London.

For more information on our books, please visit www.frontline-books.com,
email info@frontline-books.com or write to us at the above address.

Typeset by M.A.T.S. Typesetters, Leigh-on-Sea, Essex

Printed in the United States of America

CONTENTS

LIST OF ILLUSTRATIONS

Plates can be found between pages 78 and 79

FOREWORD

T HE story of the German occupation of Denmark from 1940 to 1945 is a tangled one, a story with many con- tradictions and layers. The complex narrative can be divided into three parts: the overwhelming military power subjugating a small and defenceless neighbour, the collaboration that took place, and the resistance. As for the whole war, the story of the Danish occupation carries within it many tales of humiliation, human strength, courage and compassion, of collective and individual acts of bravery, and of altruism amidst brutality, destruction and moral relativism.

The Resistance movement began its work early on in the war, but in August 1943 matters reached a turning point. General strikes broke out in many towns and cities. The population gave a clear signal that the days of ambiguity had to end. The government stood down and the leaders of the Resist- ance movement increasingly led Denmark into the Allied camp.

In October 1943 the occupiers attempted to deport the Danish Jews. It is a source of pride to many Danes, that by far the largest part of our Jewish compatriots were helped by neighbours and other ordinary citizens to escape across the sea to neighbouring Sweden. The Resistance movement was warned, by individual Germans who had inside information about the impending operation, only days before the planned deportation.

Through strikes, defiance at work sites, and damage to physical property, non-violent resisters attacked the economic interests of the invaders. Through underground publishing, an alternate network of communication was established to subvert the lies of the occupiers' propaganda. By involving so many civilians in strikes, demonstrations, and other forms of opposition, Danish resisters forced the Germans to stop the most violent reprisals, as they understood the German need to maintain normality in Denmark as much as possible.

David Lampe's book is as relevant today as when it was first written. It describes the experiences of individuals who, almost as a matter of course, risked their lives to defy the Nazis in Denmark. It tells of their bravery, courage, and selflessness. Still today, Danes, Brits and many others risk their lives almost as a matter of course. They do so to protect us from seeing Afghanistan again becoming a basis for terrorism aimed at our societies.

'Courage is resistance to fear, mastery of fear – not absence of fear', wrote Ernest Hemingway in 1942. Other tales about great courage and bravery could have been recounted. But each of the stories in this book tells of individuals, common citizens, who, when humanity and civility are threatened, defy the danger to defeat tyranny and oppression.

Apart from being truly fascinating and readable accounts of Second World War heroism, these stories also help us to better understand some of the mechanisms that induce ordinary people to overcome and master fear under extreme conditions.

AMBASSADOR BIRGER RIIS-JØRGENSEN
London, 2010

AUTHOR'S INTRODUCTION

THIS book is about a strange and little-known part of the Second World War; it concerns Denmark's resistance to five years of German occupation. It does not pretend to be either a formal history of that occupation or a complete catalogue of Resistance activity, organized or individual. Its subject has contemporary interest, for these stories—all of them true—point to the conclusion that even the smallest and least prepared country is not beaten simply because foreign troops overwhelm it—not, at least, while there are private places in which to scheme and people to do the scheming.

Without resistance, Denmark would have had an easier war, but from the beginning individual Danes felt they must do something to preserve their national self-respect. Slow in starting, they eventually produced Europe's prototype Resistance organization, good enough to earn Field-Marshal Montgomery's praise; he called it 'second to none'. It alone placed Denmark on the list of Allied nations that defeated Hitler. Much of its success stemmed from the fact that, although the Germans never learned to understand the Danish mentality, from the beginning the Danes understood the Germans.

The Wehrmacht claimed to be moving into Denmark to protect it against British invasion. In the process, the Germans said, two friendly Aryan neighbours would be united. According to a story still popular in Copenhagen, King Christian told Hitler, 'Really, I'm much too old to take on the added responsibility of ruling Germany, too.'

The Nazis permitted the Danish Government to remain in

office, and at first neither Denmark's police nor military were entirely disbanded. Disappointed when they later allowed the Danes a free election and no Quisling emerged victorious, the Nazis more realistically arranged to benefit from the little country's high farm output, and from the fact that its shipyards and precision engineering factories were unlikely to be bombed.

Denmark, alone of all the occupied countries, could not boast of a government-in-exile. It had no distinctively uniformed 'free forces' fighting alongside the Allies. In the beginning the West had had to abandon the Danes, and the Danish Resistance was unique in that it grew at first with no outside encouragement.

The most effective Resistance acts in Denmark were often apparent only to their protagonists—and, of course, very painfully, to the victims, the Germans. When former members of the Wehrmacht forces in Denmark today deny knowing at the time that they were members of an occupation army—and many of them make this incredible claim—they are lying. But, these days, when many young Danes state that they believe that their country played little part in the war, it is usually because they are unaware of how much happened. Like most casualty figures, those of Denmark's Resistance give no true idea how effective its fighting organizations were.

In any case, not all Danish resistance was organized. Danish labourers who dumped pounds of sugar into the cement they mixed for German gun emplacements, making them crumble the first time the gun fired, were not organized. Neither was the Copenhagen postman who scrutinized all letters he was supposed to deliver to the capital's Gestapo headquarters—and tore up those he suspected were from informers. Royal Air Force roundels were worn by many thousands of Danes to taunt the Germans, and nobody organized this. It was not organization that made Danish factory managers accept German production orders, either to forward the blueprints to Britain or to produce goods on assembly lines on which the final stage was invariably sabotage.

.   .   .   .   .

To write this book I needed considerable help. Ebbe Munck, whose liaison office in Stockholm was one of the most vital parts of the Danish Resistance, probably knows more about the subject personally than any other single individual, and he directed me to many of the people I interviewed. Then, as my manuscript took form, he made many constructive suggestions.

Mogens Staffeldt, at first an important contact man between the various Copenhagen resistance cells, and later Ebbe Munck's *aide*, was also particularly helpful to me from the beginning.

Among the others who assisted me were Poul Andersen and his family, Jørgen Benzon, Ingolf Boisen, Allan Blanner, Dr. Fritz Buchthal, Leo Buschardt, the Bunch-Christensen family, Dr. Thøger Busk, Commander Hassager Christiansen, Arne Duus-Hansen, the Fiil family, Major-General Sir Colin Gubbins, Werner Gyberg, Colonel Volmer Gyth, Police Chief Johannes Hansen, Leif Hendil, Dr. Jørgen Hæstrup, Stig Jensen, Flemming Juncker, H. H. Koch, Henrik Kraft, Dr. K. H. Køster, Captain Erik Larsen, Jens Lillelund, Ole Lippmann, Niels Frederik Madsen, Julius Margolinsky, Chief Rabbi Marcus Melchior, Carl Næsh-Hendriksen, Dr. H. Christian Olsen, Detective Inspector Roland Olsen, Børge Outze, Captain Keld Petersen, Ruth Philipsen, Frank Pinnock, Professor Brandt Rehberg, Dr. Stefan Rozental, Pastor Harald Sandbæk, Helga von Seck, Svenn Seehusen, Arne Sejr, Squadron-Leader Ted Sismore, Thomas Sneum, Commander Erik Stærmose, Criminal Commissioner Pehr Synnerman, Colonel Sørensen of the Copenhagen Military Hospital, Hans Edvard Teglers, Captain Børge Thing, Anton Toldstrup, Svend Truelsen, Jørgen Turin, and the officers of the Bornholm Steamship Company, the Danish-French Steamship Company, the Danish State Railways, Minerva Films A/S, the E. M. Svitzer Salvage

Company, the Freedom Museum in Copenhagen, and the Danish State Archives.

At various times documents were translated for me by Dorte Askegaard, Hanne Larsen, Bengt Petersen, John Thompson, and Inge Vestergaard.

John Sundell of Cassell & Co Ltd. was a remarkably patient and helpful editor.

DAVID LAMPE
1957

MAP OF DENMARK
AND ITS NEIGHBOURS, 1940

1
Paper Bullets

BEFORE breakfast on 9th April, 1940, the German Army invaded Denmark. The low-flying Luftwaffe bombers that sprinkled leaflets ordering the people of Copenhagen to go about their business also carried high-explosive bombs to loose on the capital if King Christian rejected Hitler's surrender ultimatum. In South Jutland a few German soldiers were spattered by Danish machine-gun fire, but for the most part the Nazis rumbled easily across Denmark in tanks and lorries, their foot troops stealing bicycles along the way. This was a small-scale blitzkrieg; the Wehrmacht were in a hurry to carry out Hitler's order to turn a land of four million Danes into a 'model protectorate'. Winston Churchill was more to the point when he later said Denmark was to be 'the sadistic murderer's canary'.

Four hours after the first Nazis entered Copenhagen seventeen-year-old Arne Sejr and some of his grammar school friends were on the city's streets distributing sixteen copies of a leaflet they had prepared. Paraphrasing the Ten Commandments, it read:

1. You must not go to work in Germany or Norway.
2. You must work badly for the Germans.
3. You must work slowly for the Germans.
4. You must spoil their production machines and tools.
5. You must spoil whatever helps the Germans.
6. You must delay all German transports.

7.   You must boycott all Italian films and papers.
8.   You must not buy or trade with the Nazis.
9.   You must treat all traitors as they deserve to be treated.
10.   You must defend every person persecuted by the Germans.
      JOIN THE FIGHT FOR DENMARK'S FREEDOM!

At that moment Sejr's friends had no idea what actions they would take next. Nevertheless, their prophetic commandments were to have a noticeable influence. The canary had begun to show eagle's claws.

Hardly more than a dozen such illegal leaflets were distributed during the first year of the occupation, for most Danes had been stunned into indolence. Hoping to cajole the Danish Press into submission, the Germans cautiously avoided imposing direct censorship, and Danes at first were satisfied to read the watered-down news in the supervised Press. In Hillerød, twenty miles north of Copenhagen, an underground newspaper began publication in May 1941 but ceased in July. When Russia joined the Allies in June 1941 the Danish Communist Press was banned, and *Land og Folk* emerged. At one period of the war *Land og Folk* secretly printed editions in twenty-one Danish cities as well as in five different sections of Copenhagen. Its production was so perfectly concealed that it spoke uninterruptedly for Danish Communists throughout the war.

In July 1942 *Studenternes Efterretningstjenste* (roughly, 'Students' Enlightenment Service') was published for the first time by young Arne Sejr's friends. One of the most powerful cells in the Resistance, the students' group had few members older than twenty-five, and most were about twenty-one. At first, their news-sheet appeared irregularly, but by 1943 it was published at regular fortnightly intervals in thirteen different Copenhagen editions and in cities in every part of

Denmark as well as on the island of Bornholm. In 1943 it engaged the pre-war proprietor of a small Copenhagen news syndicate to do liaison work with journalists all over the country. The only other staff member who was older than the students was Karl Bjarnhof, a Danish broadcaster. Bjarnhof attended all the staff meetings as recording secretary, taking notes in a shorthand only he could decipher. His risks were great. In addition to being a celebrity, he was totally blind and the notes he kept for the students were in his private Braille shorthand. By the beginning of 1944, *Studenternes Efterretnings-tjenste* had reached a peak circulation of 120,000. Although in April 1944 the Nazis succeeded in trapping a large part of its staff, the paper, with its circulation reduced to 80,000, continued to appear regularly until the liberation.

Accurate up-to-the-minute war news was published in the secret newspapers along with maps and photographs. Banned political and religious opinions found full voice. Editors were captured, tortured, and sometimes executed, but their newspapers continued to publish in attics and caves, in country villas and in city flats and offices. Before the Nazis commandeered all the rooms of Dagmarhus, a building in the Copenhagen Town Hall Square, a resistance newspaper was regularly printed on a duplicating machine on a lower floor while Nazi office typewriters clattered upstairs.

Danish saboteurs attacked German Army installations and pro-Nazi local businesses, entire cities went on strike against occupation rule, and the Danish Government resigned, to be replaced by the secret Freedom Council. All these things were reported in the clandestine papers. Many of the Resistance papers were produced entirely by amateurs. Others were the part-time work of professional journalists who remained with the authorized newspapers to keep access to story sources. News items were snatched from the wastebaskets of the German Press supervisors. Loyal Danish police and other government officials provided reports, and every Dane who knew anything the Germans wanted kept secret told the Resistance Press about it.

The newspapers' individual circulations were sometimes as high as 150,000 copies, and throughout the war more than 600 such newspapers published a total of about 26 million copies. Copenhagen alone, at one time or another, had several hundred Resistance newspapers. Sent out in bundles to be redistributed by trusted people, posted in the guise of letters, bills, or advertisements, the newspapers were read carefully and then passed on.

When they could, the illegal publishers paid for their papers themselves, and sometimes the readers gave money. The papers were always distributed free, although they sometimes sold illustrated supplements. From the beginning, however, their largest source of income was from the sale of Nazi-banned books, published secretly and sold either by students or ordinary booksellers. From international best-sellers, like Wendell Willkie's *One World* and John Steinbeck's *The Moon is Down*, to books by popular Danish authors, 438 different titles were published. Nearly every Danish printer managed to produce illegal books, although the earliest volumes were cranked out on office duplicators. There was even a cookery book—not an ordinary book of recipes but formulæ for home-made explosives and instruction in sabotage techniques.

One of the best-selling illegal books was printed in German. It was *Führerwörte*, containing quotations from Hitler's speeches delivered between 1939 and 1943. It sold 20,000 copies, mostly to German troops in Denmark. Another illegal book in German was a pocket diary, the bulk of its pages photographically reproduced from the diary most often carried by German soldiers. But the final pages of its ready-reference section were printed in small type on onionskin paper in order to appear outwardly unobtrusive. Detailed instructions were presented on those pages for feigning illness. A doctor's prescription was reproduced which the German troops could copy themselves and present at any Danish chemist's shop to get a 'medicine' guaranteed to induce incapacity.

To raise money for the Press, Danish film producers contrived to get hold of Nazi-banned films to show secretly. Most private photography was outlawed by the Germans, but the Danes made a pictorial record of everything the invaders did. One Danish film producer, arrested for showing illegal films, was sent to the Nazi-created Frøslev Concentration Camp. The result was hardly what the Germans intended, for a ciné-camera was smuggled in to him and he shot scenes of the daily life in the camp. The clandestine reels taken during the occupation—altogether about a quarter of a million feet—have been used in two documentaries produced in Denmark since the war.

Considering the extreme difficulties under which they were produced, the standard of the underground newspapers was remarkable, as was the ingenuity shown by the men who laboured night and day so that their fellow citizens might be kept aware of the true course of events in their own country and in the world at large. There was even, for the blind, a resistance newspaper in Braille.

The difficulties they struggled against only seemed to spur the editors and publishers on to new enterprise. There was, for instance, the case of the R.A.F. pilot who, having crash-landed in Denmark and been rescued, as were many other Allied airmen, by Resistance agents, remarked that he had never seen a Nazi at close range. His Resistance friends said they would see what they could do. The following day a photograph appeared on the front pages of many of the Resistance newspapers. Its caption explained that it showed a Royal Air Force officer having drinks with Nazi officers on the terrace of the Hotel d'Angleterre in Copenhagen the day before. 'He is now back in England flying for the R.A.F.'

After D-Day in Normandy, one paper, *De Frie Danske*,

celebrated the occasion by bringing out an edition in full colour.

On 29th August, 1943, Dr. Werner Best, the chief Nazi administrator in Denmark, told a meeting of Danish Press representatives in Copenhagen: 'Every editor will be answerable with his life for further attempts to poison the popular mind. . . .' In the same month Børge Outze, a crime reporter on a large Copenhagen newspaper, began carrying a gun. Outze had covered many first-rate stories the Germans would not allow to be printed, and he was tired of telling stories in innuendo. The illegal Press seemed the only medium left, but it was badly co-ordinated. Outze decided that the Resistance needed a central news agency, so he created *Information*, the only underground Press service in any Nazi-occupied country.

Outze began issuing a daily news letter and photographs from Copenhagen which he sent at first to a list of eighteen illegal newspapers all over Denmark. He also wanted *Information*'s dispatches to be published abroad, so *Information* established a Stockholm bureau. Some of *Information*'s stories were too secret even for the underground Press, but they kept Resistance editors informed in the same way that secret Press conferences helped editors in the free countries keep in touch with military operations. An elaborate code system was arranged so that the daily bulletin's bare, uncoloured stories would be understood by their recipients. At least six Resistance papers daily reprinted the entire bulletin. Others merely printed excerpts from it.

Information became a vast news pool. It relayed stories which were first printed in the more remote illegal newspapers, received news from official Danish sources, was a news outlet for the Freedom Council, and sometimes was given the chance actually to see spot news being made. A liquidation group chief might invite Outze a week in advance to come and see an informer shot, or a sabotage group would telephone an invitation to watch an explosion. As *Information* grew it was asked to watch more such things than its staff could hope to cover. At times Børge Outze, calling his local police contacts to verify stories, would find that the crime he was trying to investigate had not yet occurred or had not yet been reported. Then Outze would have to explain his 'misunderstanding' as gracefully as possible.

The Germans knew *Information* existed and often saw it. They tried constantly to destroy it, and four of *Information's* staff were executed by them during the years of occupation. When the service's staff increased to about ten people it had to have editorial conferences in the most outlandish places. One summer day the staff gathered in Tivoli, the pleasure garden in the centre of Copenhagen. An informer had warned the Nazis of the meeting, and a police cordon captured all of the staff except Outze. He worked his way into the crowd and escaped through one of Tivoli's many side entrances.

Outze went to see Stig Jensen, a portly Danish journalist and one of the early underground operators, a man who took part in nearly every sort of Resistance activity from the beginning to the end of the occupation.

'We've *got* to have a paper out this evening,' Outze explained. *Information* always had to be produced to a definite schedule to be put on the trains, boats, and aeroplanes that took it to its subscribers. Jensen suggested they should visit an old lady who duplicated theatrical scripts for Copenhagen's dramatic companies. The old woman, told that Outze was a textile merchant who wanted to circularize the Danish Parliament the next day to try to get a private bill passed to benefit his business, allowed the two journalists to use her duplicator.

While they were at work a well-known Danish journalist who knew Jensen but not Outze came to visit the old lady. He watched Outze feverishly typing the daily news bulletin directly on a stencil and asked Jensen what was happening. Jensen repeated the textile story.

'Tell your friend to leave the textile branch and become a journalist,' the newspaper man advised.

The agency occupied twenty-seven different offices during the war, and its members had to remain constantly on the alert. Whenever Outze dined in a Copenhagen restaurant he had to caution the head waiter to allow no one to leave the dining-room or to use the telephone until he departed. Often he had to get up from unfinished meals because a suspicious-looking person entered the room. He never wore his pistol openly, of course, and he is not a frightening-looking man, but Danes sensed that he was from the underground, and in restaurants they always moved as far as they could from his table to be out of the line of fire in case of trouble.

Information maintained a post office box in Copenhagen and with the help of Resistance agents employed by the state telephone service it was also given a secret telephone line. Whenever members of the staff or their contacts were caught by the Germans, the office moved and the telephone number was changed.

Information's mailing list grew to several hundred names and had to be concealed carefully; it was a key to the entire Danish Resistance Press. Outze himself memorized the list and recited it every day to the people addressing envelopes for him. Soon it became apparent that this was risky, because if anything happened to the editor, his news service would stop.

For a time the list was written in sections, and these were concealed in unlikely places all over Copenhagen. At one time they were kept in a room full of deadly bacteria in the Copenhagen Serum Institute. Then the list was written phonetically in an obscure Arabian dialect by a Dane who had travelled in the East. Addressing envelopes for more than one day's mailing was never safe. And the service limited its list to a thousand subscribers.

Many of *Information*'s best stories came from Germany. *Information*, not Dr. Otto John, was first to report the Peenemünde rocket launching station to the Allies. When the first V-1 fell accidentally on Bornholm, the Danish island off Sweden's south coast, *Information* relayed technical details of the bomb to British Intelligence long before the first V-1 was aimed at London. Another dispatch told how, late in the war, all sorts of Danish ships slipped through the Nazi sea blockade to be interned in Sweden where they later would help transport across the Sound the 5,000 armed, uniformed members of the Danish Brigade, if they were needed to fight during the liberation.

Sometimes *Information* created new illegal papers in areas of Denmark were none existed. The bulletin would regularly be sent to a responsible local person. Unable to refrain from relating what he knew, this person would eventually start a newspaper.

Getting the dispatches to *Information*'s Stockholm bureau was important; from there they were relayed to the Associated Press, Reuter's, and Tass to be sent all over the world. Although the Danish underground's radio link with Sweden was strong, getting priority to transmit *Information*'s bulletins, most of which were not military, was rarely possible until the last days of the war. Sometimes the dispatches were taped underneath a German goods waggon crossing on the Elsinore-Helsingborg boat-train. The number of the waggon was radioed in code to Swedish friends of the Danish Resistance who met the train and picked up the dispatches. Copies of *Information* were carried to Sweden inside hollow pencils or inside fountain pens. The Resistance boats that regularly crossed to Sweden often carried them. Sometimes the daily letter was sent to Sweden on the German airliner that stopped at Kastrup Airport, Copenhagen, on its scheduled flight between Berlin and Stockholm. The chocks used to brake the Lufthansa aircraft at Kastrup were hollow and Outze's mimeographed dispatches were sealed inside the wooden wedges. These were thrown aboard the aircraft by Resistance workers and Danish agents in Sweden would unload the aeroplanes and put aside the chocks. The Germans never realized that they were helping the illegal Press get stories out of Denmark.

At first *Information*'s letters were distributed free, but later its subscribers were asked to pay thirty kroner a month to help cover the mailing and other expenses, and towards the end of the war the Freedom Council helped get a secret appropriation from the Danish Government to help subsidize the bulletin.

In October 1944, Børge Outze was captured by the Germans and questioned continually in Shell House, the Copenhagen Gestapo headquarters. He was to be executed. Outze spun his captors a story about a mythical agreement made between the western Allies and Russia. He said that Russia had promised not to advance westward beyond a certain line which he drew on a map for the Germans. Because the Russians had crossed his fictional line, Outze said, he would work for the Germans against the Soviets. On the strength of this absurd story the Germans released him. But from the time of Outze's imprisonment until the liberation *Information* had to be produced by other Danish journalists. Altogether it published a total of 575 daily bulletins during the war.

On the chance that the normal Danish Press would not be able to publish immediately at the end of the war, plans were made to turn *Information* into a daily newspaper, and a standby portable power station was made ready to turn its presses if other power supplies were cut. The first edition announced Denmark's liberation.

Originally, the paper was to have lasted only until the first post-war Danish cabinet was elected in August 1945, but the newspaper was allowed to continue, and Børge Outze still edits it from the premises used during the war by Denmark's Nazi newspaper.

The Nazis tried to debase the underground Press by publishing false newspapers and leaflets purportedly produced by the Resistance, but Danes were never fooled.

However, as Jens Lillelund, a Copenhagen businessman-turned-saboteur said in 1940: 'The British are not fighting the Germans with newspapers. Something more positive will have to be done in Denmark.'

2
The Deserters

FROM the beginning a few Danes were unwilling to sit out the war at home in neutrality. An opera singer swam the Sound, and in the winter of 1940 some people walked across the frozen water to Sweden. But no escape was more improbable than the one engineered by Second-Lieutenant Thomas C. Sneum, a Royal Danish Fleet Air Arm fighter pilot at a south Sealand base.

Weeks before the Germans came Sneum had tried to get nine of his fellow officers to fly their aeroplanes with his to northern Sweden, but their commanding officer forbade their leaving. When the Germans came, Sneum and his friends ignored the first order of General Kaupisch, Commandant of German Troops in Denmark, that '. . . the army and navy will show a spirit of understanding . . . by desisting from any passive or active resistance. . . .' Sneum and his friends deserted their air station. 'Such resistance,' Kaupisch's order had also threatened, 'would be unavailing and broken by all forcible means. . . .'

On his own initiative, Sneum began collecting information about German tactical positions in Denmark. In May 1940 he was told that German searchlight batteries on the west coast island of Fanø could detect oncoming aircraft before the aeroplane appeared over the horizon. The twenty-six-year-old officer was eager to convey this and other information to the British, so he located a boat in Jutland that could carry him and his friends to England. But by the time they were ready to depart the winter ice made the trip unfeasible, so Sneum sent his intelligence data with another Danish naval pilot, Kai Oxlund, who was escaping to Sweden. Then, in February 1941, Sneum fled across the Sound by boat to present more information to the British authorities in Stockholm. They agreed to try Sneum's plan to land a Sunderland flying-boat on Lake Tissø in Denmark. There Sneum would muster about twenty of his fellow officers to await evacuation to Britain. Returning to Denmark early in the spring of 1941 Sneum shot some ciné-film of the German installations on Fanø; he did not know it, but he was photographing a Nazi radar station.

When the British did not send the flying-boat, Sneum and his friends decided to escape to England in Sneum's boat, but by then the Germans were tightly patrolling the Danish coasts. Some of the other officers escaped to Sweden, and some merged into the Danish civil population. Sneum and twenty--four-year-old Keld Petersen alone decided to find a way to get directly to England. Had they gone to Sweden at that time they might have been interned, so they would have to get directly from Denmark to Britain. Until then, no Dane had succeeded in doing this.

In the civil aviation ministry's files in Copenhagen Sneum found records of about twenty-five privately-owned aircraft in Denmark, and on Whit Sunday 1941 he took a train to Odense where, outside the city, he found Elseminde, the large dairy farm of Poul Andersen.

'Mr. Andersen, my name is Petersen. I'm a civil-engineer from Copenhagen,' Sneum said. 'I understand you have an aeroplane for sale.'

Poul Andersen shook his head. 'I have a Hornet Moth—but not for sale. It was at Kastrup on April the ninth, and the Germans made me take its wings off and ship it back here by train. But even if you could put my plane together, and even if I were to sell it to you, and even if you could make it fly'— he began to close the door—'the Germans wouldn't let you use it. Good day.'

Sneum's pale eyes twinkled. 'Not for sale even if it's going to England?' he asked slyly.

Andersen hastily invited Sneum into his house where the pilot identified himself and explained why he needed the aircraft. 'Lieutenant Sneum, your problem is solved,' Andersen said finally. 'I don't want to sell the machine, but it's at your disposal.'

At dusk the pair moved stealthily to a small corrugated-iron, T-shaped hangar at the edge of a turnip field; German infantrymen were in a nearby copse. Even in the dim light Sneum could tell that putting the aeroplane together would be difficult. The bolts that had held the struts and wings in place had been lost and the rudder pedals were gone, too. The Hornet Moth's tail fin had been smashed and would have to be rebuilt. There would be no chance to warm up the engine, much less to make even the most rudimentary tests that all newly assembled aircraft should have before being used for prolonged flights.

The plane would have to appear to have been stolen, so neither Sneum, Petersen, nor the mechanic they later brought from Copenhagen dared approach the hangar in daylight. Always they had to work silently by torchlight. Curious German troops might wander into the hangar at any time because they knew a dismantled aircraft was there. Andersen himself never risked approaching the building while the aeroplane was being assembled.

Often in the daytime Sneum and Petersen visited Elseminde to learn what they could about the aeroplane. Andersen told them that the large Danish flags painted on the fuselage and the undersides of the wings had been put there during the winter before the occupation when the aeroplane had taken supplies to ice-bound people in the Kattegat. Sneum decided not to paint over the flags—a decision that probably prolonged his life.

Carefully seating the wings in place, Sneum, Petersen, and their helper tightened bolts that had been made secretly in an Odense factory, atop the worn, dark-grey circles the original

bolts' washers had made when first the silver-coloured aeroplane had been assembled. There was no way to tell if the
crisscrossed wires between the wings were drawn to the correct
tension. Sneum decided not to bother to improvise rudder
pedals because the Moth would have to make just one landing.

Sometimes the three men heard the German soldiers
thrashing through the field outside the hangar. The
mechanic and Petersen would grin nervously, but Sneum
would shrug his shoulders and probe around with the torch
beam to find the next part that needed fitting. The
aeroplane's assembly took three weeks. Sneum planned to
make the flight on the night of 20th June, but the aeroplane
was not quite ready, and when he, Petersen, and the
mechanic trudged into Odense that night they passed a
German artillery unit moving 37-mm. anti-aircraft guns past
the farm. Had they flown off in the Hornet Moth that
night, they would almost certainly have been shot down.

Foot-high turnip-tops fringed the nubby field outside the
hangar. The next field was knee-high in barley, but a third
field with only a stubble of stiff grass would be fine for the
take-off—once the plane had been taxied across the turnips
and through. the barley. German soldiers occupied houses
along the right side of that grass field—within shouting
distance. Power lines which were strung across the far end of
the field would be serious obstacles. Sneum thought that with
the weight of the fifty five-litre petrol cans he would pile
behind the seats in the aeroplane's cabin they would have to
taxi under the wires and become airborne on the downward-
dipping part of the field between the wires and the railway
tracks that cut across the bottom. He planned to use the
sound of a passing express train to cover the noise of the
Hornet Moth's Gypsy engine. They would have to escape
within sight and earshot of Wehrmacht troops.

On Saturday, 21st June, Sneum and Keld Petersen called at
the Elseminde farmhouse for the last time. Both pilots' civilian

clothes fitted bulkily over their Danish Naval uniforms. Sneum carried detailed aerial maps of Denmark, but the only map he had of Britain was torn from an atlas. Keld Petersen carried a large revolver. The sky was still bright when, an hour before midnight, Andersen went with them to the hangar; it was the time of the year in Denmark when there is not enough darkness to reduce objects on the horizon to silhouettes. The *Dannebrog* (the Danish flag) seemed almost to glisten on the side of the plane. OY-DOK, the identification letters, stood out clearly. As quietly as they could, the three men drew open the hangar doors. Because the building had been built to accommodate a smaller aeroplane, they had to fold back the wings of the Hornet Moth to roll it through the doorway. Even then they ripped the covering on the wings' leading edges, but there was no time for more repairs.

Sneum climbed into the cockpit behind the port controls. Glancing over his shoulder he saw the pile of reserve petrol cans, the siphon hose, and the broomstick and large towel they would need later. Remembering that the Hornet Moth's tanks had been nearly empty for more than a year, Sneum hoped that resins in the evaporating petrol had not gummed up the fuel filters. Nothing else—not even food—was put aboard to add extra weight.

Faint sounds of thick German voices and the sudden, heavier noise of a Wehrmacht vehicle growling along a lane, carried across the cool night air. 'Switch off' Sneum whispered. For a few minutes there was no other sound near by except Petersen's quick breathing as he turned over the propeller to lubricate and prime the aircraft's engine.

Sneum tightened his safety belt across his lap. Keld Petersen, revolver tucked in his belt, waited nervously in front of the propeller. Then from a distance came the growing chuffing of a train.

'Now! Contact!' Sneum ordered softly.

'Good luck!' whispered Andersen.

Keld Petersen reached up with both hands, grasped the edge of the propeller and flipped it down sharply. As the train neared the bottom of the grass field the Gypsy engine broke into a roar that seemed to tear the night apart. Poul Andersen crouched to pull the chocks from the wheels. Keld Petersen, waving his pistol, was already running across the turnips, trying not to stumble over the rough dirt clods and thick low foliage, leading OY-DOK toward the barley field.

Sneum worked the throttle, certain that the Germans could not miss the engine's noise. He had hoped the train would be even noisier.

Keld Petersen ran on, waving his pistol, his breath coming hard and his face taut and sweating. If the Germans came now, he felt he would shoot as many as he could and kill the rest with his bare hands.

They had apparently tinkered the aeroplane's engine into perfect tune. Still cold, it worked perfectly.

Galloping into the barley field Petersen glanced over his shoulder. The Hornet Moth's propeller fanned the barley, pulling the aircraft roughly through the thick growth. Petersen saw the crudely mended tailplane rise up and then thud down again. Crossing on to the grass he glanced right and saw German soldiers, but none of them were running towards him. In the distance sparks spurted from the railway engine. The Hornet Moth sounded louder than a bomber.

Petersen ran around the propeller and scrambled into the cockpit. Sneum opened the throttle and the plane shot forward before Petersen had time even to slam the door. Still groping for his safety belt as they left the ground, Petersen accidentally poked the broomstick through the fabric roof of the cabin. In front of them were the power lines. They were airborne more quickly than they had hoped.

Sneum pulled back the control stick hard and they rose gently. 'I don't think we can clear those wires,' he yelled. 'Hang on!'

Perfectly relaxed, Sneum eased the control carefully forward and the Moth's nose dipped. Petersen had the sensation of hunching his shoulders and trying to duck his head as they flew under the power line. Sneum drew hard on the stick again, and again the plane began to climb, seeming nearly to drag its wheels across the dipping field and over the cab of the railway engine. Less than twenty feet below Sneum noticed the driver's upturned face. They skimmed through some trees as the biplane's wings dropped clumsily from side to side.

The German soldiers saw the small aircraft hedge-hopping like an artillery spotting plane. In the monochromatic dusk the white crosses that quartered the red fields of the *Dannebrogs* made the flags look like the Luftwaffe's Maltese crosses, and the Germans must have thought that, because they did not open fire.

Sneum held the control stick as far back as it could go— almost in his lap. 'How does she fly?' Petersen asked.

'Left wing heavy,' Sneum grunted. 'The angles of incidence are all wrong and the damned nose pulls down.'

From the hangar, Poul Andersen watched the low-flying air-craft waggle its wings, heel, and then head due south. Leisurely, he turned, and walked home to his blacked-out farmhouse.

Sneum levelled into westward flight over a railway track to check the Moth's compass. In that direction it read thirty degrees off. Because they had no radio, they would have no way of knowing in advance if they were being intercepted. Their hundred-knot speed made them slow enough to be brought down by a rifleman's lucky shot, but Sneum had charted their course carefully to avoid German military posts.

A control tower of an airfield saw the tiny biplane flying over the Little Belt between Funnen and Jutland. Furiously the base flashed searchlight instructions to the Moth to land, but the two pilots did not reply. They were at 3,000 feet and entering solid cloud, and their only blind flying instrument was a turn and bank indicator. Near Haderslev, just across the Little Belt, they came out of the clouds and piloted a zig-zag course, hoping to cross the coast between the islands of Fanø and Rømø.

The Fanø radar station picked up the aircraft and vectored a fighter into the air, but the Luftwaffe pilot was unable to find the small plane.

Back in Odense, Andersen made trunk calls to friends along the Jutland coast who knew people who would report to the authorities if any aircraft were brought down. No, they said, nothing had been reported yet. Andersen waited an hour, called again, learned nothing, and finally went to bed. The German soldiers in the fields near Elseminde carried on with their training patrols all night.

The Hornet Moth's nose still tended to dip downward and Sneum had to keep the stick sharply back, and occasionally the aeroplane yawed violently. When they had a chance, the pilots slipped off their civilian clothes. There were no instrument lights in the machine, so Petersen directed his torch at the dials until their radium-tinted needles absorbed enough light to glow for about fifteen minutes. Petrol fumes escaped from the loosely-capped tins behind the seats.

An hour and a half out over the North Sea the engine began spluttering; the carburettors had iced up. Petersen's torch beam showed that the oil pressure gauge was giving no reading. Sneum had to throttle full back, then dip into a sharp glide. They both remembered they had forgotten to bring life-jackets, and they carried no parachutes. There was absolutely nothing to be done, and the altimeter suggested they were dangerously near the water. The smell of petrol was almost overpowering.

A few hundred feet over the water the engine suddenly caught. Sneum threw forward the throttle, pulled back the control stick and at last they began to roar upwards. The torchlight showed that their oil pressure was between zero and five kilograms.

After about four hours their fuel tank was almost empty. Petersen was groggy because of the petrol fumes, but Sneum told him to reach over and take the control stick. Then he opened the port-side cabin door, and as wind howled into the aeroplane he took the siphon hose and gingerly stepped out on to the wing, holding on to the cockpit door with one hand.

'For Christ's sake, Tommy, don't fall off!' Petersen yelled.

Groping along the smooth fuselage, Sneum took anxious minutes to find the fuel filler cap, prize it open, and fit the hose into the port as the plane wobbled in the air. Then he fastened himself back in his seat again. One tin at a time, sloshing the liquid everywhere and completely drenching Sneum, Petersen began funnelling petrol slowly into the hose.

A little later they came out of clouds for the first time since Fanø. By the position of the North Star they could tell they were on course. Dawn on Sunday 22nd June came brightly. More than six hours after their take-off Petersen and Sneum saw two pairs of fighter planes racing sleekly towards them— Royal Air Force Hurricanes and Spitfires. The four fighters heeled to make passes at the little silver Hornet Moth, circling around OY-DOK as if it were hanging still in the air, orbiting close, apparently to have a better look at the red and white flags and the unfamiliar identification letters. Sneum, keeping their nose pointed in what he hoped was the direction of Britain, ordered, 'Quick, Keld! Show them the white flag!'

Petersen knotted the big white towel over the broomstick and thrust it through the Perspex window at his right. He waved the towel frantically as the four fighters slipped past again and winged out of sight. The Hornet Moth was flying due south-west and a small island lay ahead. 'No sign of any kind of island on the map, Tommy,' Petersen shouted. 'This looks like the mouth of the Zuider Zee. Do you think we could be lost?'

Sneum grinned. 'I suppose we could be.'

Ahead and beneath them they could see land—Scotland,

they hoped. Actually, they had crossed the coastline south of Berwick. The island had been Coquet Island.

Sneum was busily looking for a place to land and had changed the course to what he hoped was due south. In a coastal town they saw no people below them—an air raid alert had been given when the Moth was spotted. Seeing soldiers in a camp below, Sneum decided they had better come down quickly before the British began throwing ack-ack at them.

In Odense, Mr. Andersen was out of bed and tending to his cows; in a few hours he would report that his Hornet Moth had been stolen during the night. He tuned in the B.B.C.'s Danish broadcast hoping to get news, but he heard nothing.

The Northumberland farm labourer who ran over to the Moth when it touched down heavily in his field, and rolled to a stop at the gate that opened on to a road, was frightened, especially when the taller of the two blue-uniformed blonde fliers asked, 'What place is this?'

The labourer refused to answer.

'At least you can tell us if it's England or Scotland.'

'England!' the man called over his shoulder, running to get help.

The Home Guard member who rode up on a bicycle was followed by soldiers, airmen, even armoured-cars, and the two fliers were soon on their way, under escort, to the R.A.F. station at Acklington.

In the station mess breakfast was ready, and the station intelligence officer who questioned them said they would be sent to the London clearing centre for foreign troops who entered Britain unconventionally. Eventually Sneum and Petersen were allowed to sleep.

Within five days of their landing Sneum was taken from the London clearing centre for a special assignment, and Keld Petersen was commissioned in the Royal Air Force.

· · · ·

At eight o'clock in the morning Andersen telephoned Odense police that his aeroplane had been stolen. Because a Luftwaffe pilot from a nearby base had deserted and might have taken the aircraft, the local Nazi occupation authorities at first did not question Andersen. By the time they began their investigation he had already heard a report on the B.B.C. Danish Service that two Danish airmen had arrived in England. Neither of the men's names nor the details of their escape were related. British newspapers were not permitted to mention the story.

For a year the Germans in Odense kept close watch on Poul Andersen, but they learned nothing about what had happened to his plane. During that time Andersen dared do nothing to help the underground organizations that were then budding.

3

Under a Postage Stamp

O N a six-foot map of the world the kingdom of Den-
mark can be covered by an ordinary postage stamp.
Although over a million Danes live in the
Copenhagen-Frederiksberg area, practically no places exist in
Denmark from which a dwelling cannot be seen. But to arm
the Danish Resistance, the Special Operations Executive in
Baker Street planned to parachute weapons, explosives and
other equipment into the postage-stamp country. Even before
Sneum's flight, Ebbe Munck, a Copenhagen journalist, had set
up a liaison office in Stockholm that would be the major link
between the Danish Resistance and S.O.E. By early 1943
Munck's friends in Denmark had reception groups ready. At
first mostly North Jutland peasants, they waited on the lonely
heaths, signalled the low-flying aircraft with electric torches,
gathered the few tons of material that cascaded to them on
twenty-foot parachutes, then spirited these things away—all
before the local German occupation troops, who often could
also hear the aircraft, arrived. A very dangerous business, its
early history was tragic.

One of the first groups was led by Marius Fiil, a small,
beak-nosed, fifty-year-old Jutland innkeeper whose entire
family, and a few of their neighbours in their little village of
Hvidsten, received the drops. Fiil smuggled away the material
himself in his farm cart under loads of antiques bought to
decorate his inn. Mindless of security, he hid the contraband
in a barn just across the road from his inn, and he also allowed
Danish agents parachuted by the British to stay in his house for

a few days, and, although it was risky, many of these agents returned to visit him.

When peat diggers found some of the containers and parachutes in a bog near Hvidsten, the Germans located Fiil's dropping-point, and for the next few months the innkeeper's only Resistance work was to help the escape of Allied airmen who had crashed in Denmark. But when the British decided to resume operations near Hvidsten, Fiil suggested to the local Resistance leader, Flemming Juncker, that a site even nearer Hvidsten be used. Juncker, a landowner, thought this dangerous, but Fiil was insistent; before, he said, he had had to carry the containers too far.

But after several successful receptions, German military police arrested Marius Fiil, his two young daughters, the husband of the older girl, and Fiil's son. Six of the neighbours who had helped Fiil were also caught, but the tenth man in the Hvidsten Group escaped. The Fiil sisters were sent to a concentration camp, and, in late June 1944, the nine men were executed. Other groups were by then active in North Jutland, on Sealand, and in other parts of Denmark, and other tragedies occurred, but the Danes still fearlessly awaited the air drops, despite frequent German ambushes.

On Sealand, the Copenhagen journalist who was one of Denmark's first full-time Resistance men, Stig Jensen, arranged air drop receptions. In Jutland, after Juncker had to flee to England, a young customs inspector named Anton Jensen— after the war he legally adopted his cover name of 'Toldstrup' —was chief organizer. When they were convinced of the Danish Resistance's potential, the British were eager to make as many drops as possible, and both Jensens—not relatives—began regularly to arrange the impossible.

When, for example, the British were using eight dropping-points in Jutland but wanted the locations of forty additional possible ones, each to be eight hundred metres long and isolated from view, Toldstrup snorted, 'There aren't forty places like that in all Denmark!' But a week later he sent Baker Street a list of suitable North Jutland sites. True, they were not all isolated, but all were eventually used safely—and instead of forty places, Toldstrup had suggested fifty.

Stig Jensen, once given a last-minute order to provide a reception site south of Copenhagen, realized he had no place that could be used, for his best dropping area had been raided by the Germans a few days earlier. Relying on his sense of humour and his ability to out-think the Germans, Jensen asked for the parachutage to be made on the only point he knew where the Nazis would not expect anything to be dropped. The containers were successfully received—at the exact spot where the Germans had earlier staged their raid.

Ten small villages are on the island of Samsø, south-east of Aarhus, but the total German occupation force there was only eight men. Well fed and not bothered by the islanders, these Germans were having a very pacific war. Why not, Toldstrup suggested to S.O.E., make air drops on Samsø? The containers came, and the Germans did not—or pretended they did not—notice what was happening. However, the waters around the island were mined, and getting contraband to the Jutland mainland on the Aathus-Samsø coaster was so much of a nuisance that the island's dropping point was discontinued. Several air drops were aimed at other small Danish islands, but transport was again always a problem. Worse, the containers frequently fell into the sea and had to be retrieved in the daytime.

If German troops or local farmers appeared near the dropping-points, the reception groups would not flash their Morse code letter to the aeroplanes, and the aircraft would return to Britain. But sometimes the drops were received under strange conditions. At their very first reception, men of a new group formed by Toldstrup heard the roar of an aircraft and pointed their torch up to give the 'Ready' signal. They then saw the black silhouettes of the parachutes and soon began to gather up the containers. While they were still doing this, they heard another aircraft engine, and again they flashed a signal. Again more containers dropped toward them. A third aircraft flew over, and the men in the reception group again signalled. Still more containers came down.

By that time the Resistance men found they had three times as many containers as they were prepared to handle. The second two aircraft were supposed to have made their drops elsewhere. The reception group had not finished getting all the things away before dawn, and they decided to leave most of the containers piled near a tiny village and come back for them in the evening.

At dusk they found the entire village had gathered where the containers were hidden, trying to decide what these strange objects were. The Resistance men pleaded with the villagers to go away, but the people would not leave. A horse and cart were brought to take away the containers, and all the villagers trooped after it—as if it were a funeral procession. However, all of the curious peasants were loyal Danes, and the Germans never got to hear of this episode.

Stig Jensen's men had a more harrowing experience on New Year's Eve, 1944. After receiving a last-minute wireless instruction from England to be ready at a dropping-point, Jensen marshalled his men. The aeroplane swooped low and Jensen saw the parachutes blossom, but something went wrong and one of the containers burst open before it hit the ground, scattering its contents all over a freshly ploughed field. While some of the men gathered up the unbroken containers, the other men began wading around in the cold mud. Sten guns, hand grenades and ammunition were everywhere. The men did not finish their work until daybreak, and when they had taken away everything they could find, they suddenly realized that three parachutes were missing. Searching for those in the daytime would be too risky, so they decided to go to bed.

Later that morning a farmer near the dropping-point picked up his telephone. 'I want to speak to the German commander,' he told the operator. 'There are several parachutes in front of my house, and I don't like it at all.'

'I'm sorry, sir,' the operator told him, 'but the line is out of order. I'll call you back as soon as I can.'

When the man had hung up, the operator called another number, her own house, and woke up her husband, who was one of the men Stig Jensen had ordered to wade through the field to collect the material from the burst container.

Soon Jensen arrived at the farmer's house. In a tree he saw the three missing parachutes, their containers swinging beneath them. The farmer came outside while the Resistance men were cutting down the parachutes. Jensen covered him with his pistol and ordered him to help. Using the farmer's telephone, the journalist then called for a lorry.

'M-m-may I,' the frightened farmer asked, 'have one of the parachutes?'

Jensen grinned. 'Of course you may,' and added, 'But remember, if the Germans catch you with it, they'll shoot you; and if you tell the Germans about it, then *we'll* shoot you!'

After the Resistance men had driven away, the farmer rushed into his house, picked up his telephone, and told the operator, 'You don't have to call the Germans for me. I was mistaken. That matter has been taken care of.'

Another time an aircraft looking for its dropping-area in southern Sealand saw lights on the ground, and the pilot signalled his crew to push out the containers. The parachutes fell toward the lights, but the men below were very surprised, for the pilot had missed his dropping-area and had loosed twenty-four containers on a railway goods yard. The men with the lights had been German troops shunting trains.

Once a young boy in a Jutland village was out on an errand after dark, and when he heard a low-flying aircraft, he pointed his torch at the sky and flashed it on and off. Suddenly the boy saw parachutes, and containers began plummeting all around him. Toldstrup's men, at a dropping-point not far from the village, soon were told what had happened and sped towards the town. However, the Germans had also already been alerted to the drop, and they in their turn hurried to the area. Unfortunately, the latter party won the race by a few minutes, and only one of the containers could be retrieved.

In Sealand, Stig Jensen's men once went out for a reception on a winter night in 1944, and when they heard an aeroplane fly near, Jensen flashed his signal. Instead of containers coming down, tracer bullets began to rain around the Resistance men. By mistake Jensen had signalled a Luftwaffe fighter on patrol.

The Danes on the ground took cover in a drainage ditch, and a few minutes later the British aircraft arrived and had to enter into a dogfight over the dropping area. Waist-deep in water, Jensen's reception group peered up at the aerial battle above them. The British aeroplane burst into flames, and its crew and the Danish parachutist it carried had to bale out. Jensen was later able to get the officers from the aircraft to safety, but the non-commissioned men were taken by the Germans. The Danish parachutist spent the night hidden in a haystack, and made his way to Copenhagen in the morning.

Most of the receptions were more successful, however, and the much bigger problem was carrying away the containers. Here, Danish ingenuity again proved itself. Sometimes doctors' cars were used because they could travel about freely. In North Jutland a hearse cruised back and forth across the countryside at night, its flowers and wreaths concealing loads of air-dropped goods. But such means of transport were risky, because the Danes who saw them were likely either to gossip about them or to be caught by the Germans and made to talk. For a long time Toldstrup's men carried away explosives under a large load of logs in a lorry, but this disguise was eventually penetrated by a German road patrol. A final answer had to be found to the transport problem—and eventually one of Toldstrup's men worked out the perfect solution.

The Resistance men bought a large removals van, and travelling from auction to auction, purchased several dozen pieces of old furniture. With their explosives and weapons in the front part of the van, the furniture would be packed tightly at the back. If the doors were opened by curious Germans, some of the furniture would tumble to the road. The Germans stopped this van many times but could never be bothered to take out enough of the chairs and tables to find the hidden contraband.

Almost from the first, men sometimes came down with the containers; S.O.E.-trained agents, Danes who were to be the cadre of the entire Danish Resistance. Each of them carried a poison he was to swallow if the Germans caught him and tried to torture him into yielding information, and each was worth a 20,000-kroner reward to Danes who disclosed his where-abouts to the Nazis. Except for these two facts, the agents had little in common. Some were weak characters who had taken on the job because a commission and the pay of a British Army officer went with it. Some were opportunists who squandered the large sums of money they had been entrusted to deliver to Resistance workers forced underground. One of these agents went on a drinking spree in Copenhagen and told chance acquaintances about his secret work. He was having so much fun in the occupied city that he would not obey an S.O.E. order to go to Sweden—and he had to be liquidated.

On the day of Copenhagen's liberation one of the first parachutists who had been received by the Hvidsten Group strutted the streets of the capital in a British officer's uniform. He had earlier been captured by the Germans and later released. It is known that he was threatened with torture, but was never actually tortured. He never tried to take his own life. In addition to the Hvidsten Group, it is believed that he gave the Germans the names of at least seventy Resistance people.

Another man received by the Fiils was a nineteen-year-old who brought poison tablets with him instead of a phial of liquid because, he told his hosts, he was afraid broken glass would cut his tongue. His tablets were effective; captured, he used them to take his life.

A few of the agents had lived so long outside Denmark that they at first had trouble remaining inconspicuous. Too many were peasant types, completely unable to command authority over the underground volunteers they were supposed to lead. Some were either brave or highly honourable or resourceful— but few showed all these qualities until later in the war when the Danes were able to send men back to Britain to be trained and returned to Denmark. Yet despite the antipathy so many Danes in England at first felt towards irregular fighting at home, some of the first agents were excellent men.

In the summer of 1943 one of these parachutists landed in Jutland with some strange equipment built into a suitcase not much larger than a portable typewriter. It was something the Danes had never seen before, and the parachutist showed them how to use it. He did not explain its precise purpose, but the Danes soon guessed. Known as a Eureka station, it was a battery-powered wireless receiver and transmitter. Eventually eleven more similar pieces of equipment were parachuted into Jutland, and later four larger Eureka stations were also dropped there.

The British sent Toldstrup precise orders about where to set up the Eurekas and when to work them. Switching on the instruments, their operators would listen on earphones until they heard a steady buzzing. Then they would begin tapping out a single letter in Morse code—whichever letter the British specified. Until the buzz in their earphones died away, the operators sent out the same letter again and again. The smaller sets were moved from place to place to avoid detection by the

Germans, but the four larger stations were fixed permanently in church steeples along the west coast of Jutland. The Eurekas were beacons that helped Allied aircraft pick their way toward dropping-areas, but they were being used as more than just an aid to the Danish Resistance. During the last year of the war, when large-scale air raids were being made on Germany, British and American bombers had to fly back and forth over Denmark, although the Germans had many active anti-aircraft stations there. Without knowing it at the time, the Danish Resistance helped make bombardment of the Reich a little less hazardous for the Allied airmen.

All the Eureka stations were equipped with high explosive charges that could be detonated to destroy them if they were captured, but the operators Toldstrup put in charge of the sets did their job well, and none was ever discovered.

More air-dropped goods were lost to the Germans in raids on storage places than were lost in faulty drops or in transit. One of the strangest storage systems was employed by a North Jutland blacksmith. His neighbours all knew he was a Resistance man—such things could not be kept secret in Jutland's smaller, more remote villages—but he had his own technique for keeping down loose talk. If he learned that someone had mentioned his activities, he would take them aside, prop one foot on a chair, draw up his trouser leg, and reveal the pistol he always carried strapped to his calf. 'Have you been talking?' he would ask.

'No, no!' the worried villager would protest.

Unstrapping his pistol, the blacksmith would then point it at his neighbour. 'Tell the truth or I'll kill you!'

'Well, yes, I suppose I have said a little.'

'Next time you talk, I won't show this to you. I'll use it!'

His neighbours all became close-mouthed, and the smith kept the air-dropped things openly on the shelves of his shop.

'If somebody came in for plastic explosive,' he later explained, 'I didn't want him to go off with nuts and bolts, so I marked the packages "plastic explosive".'

After the invasion of France the air drops to Denmark increased; many containers that had been earmarked for the Maquis began to find their way to Denmark instead. The first containers that had been dropped into North Jutland while Flemming Juncker was still in command there often held cigarettes and other small gifts for the people who risked their lives to receive the contraband, but Juncker had sent radio messages to England that such kindnesses might inadvertently betray the Resistance. Cigarettes began to appear again in the containers towards the end of the war. But they were not likely to be noticed by the Germans, for they were black, French-type cigarettes—and the Danes hated them.

Early in 1945 the Royal Air Force decided to experiment with a new dropping technique in Jutland, and Toldstrup was asked to provide very strange dropping points that would not require men to await the aeroplanes. Several such operations were carried out. The containers were plummeted into the sea where they sank and anchored themselves at the bottom along uninhabited parts of the Jutland coast. The only trace was a small marker buoy bobbing on the surface. The day after these drops, Resistance men went out in small boats and jerked on the buoys, releasing a mechanism attached to the anchors. The containers would bob to the surface and could be taken away safely—as long as no one observed the boats. No such drops were made elsewhere in Europe, and Toldstrup suggested to the British that the operations would be even more perfect if the buoys were made to look like small sea birds. But the war ended before this idea could be tried.

During the last days of the war drops were so prevalent in Jutland that Toldstrup had not forty or fifty but more than three hundred dropping sites in operation, and on the night the

Germans in Denmark capitulated, ninety-three drops were to have been made in that part of the country.

Stig Jensen also planned his most ambitious reception for a night in May 1945. He had arranged to have eighteen goods waggons drawn to a siding in South Sealand. Next to the railway line was the dropping area, and the R.A.F. was going to throw down enough containers to fill the entire train. Every detail of the operation was carefully worked out. It was only called off because it was scheduled for a night nearly a week after British troops took over Copenhagen.

4

Two Thousand Bangs

FREDERIKSBERG is a separate city adjacent to Copenhagen, but the business sections of the two intermingle. The Forum on Rosenørns Allé in Frederiksberg is the largest exhibition hall in Scandinavia, and on 25th August, 1943, it was to have become a German Army barracks.

The day before, shortly after the workmen converting the building had cycled away for lunch, a delivery boy pedalled up to the back entrance, a case apparently containing Tuborg beer on the underslung carrier of what Danes call a Long John bicycle. Two more men, dressed as labourers, cycled to the kerb and waited as another pair of men stepped from a taxi and entered the building. In the back seat of the taxi a sixth man gripped a sub-machine gun. When the Danish foreman and watchman had been routed from the Forum at pistol point, the delivery boy took his Tuborg crate inside the hall. Under the empty bottles were more than a hundred pounds of marzipan-smelling P-3 explosive. The leader of the men, a commercial artist named Tom Søndergaard, went back into the building to make sure no one was still inside, and a few minutes later, believing the building to be empty, the young cyclist lit the two-minute fuze on his bomb and fled from the Forum on his bicycle. Just as the second of the saboteurs, Jens Lillelund, was about to hurry away on his bicycle he noticed that Søndergaard had not come out. Lanky, bald Lillelund was within ten feet of the doorway when his whole world filled with a jarring, shattering blast. The Forum's cement-block walls pulverized like sugar, leaving only a splintering, cobweb steel skeleton, and slivers of glass tied in the dusty rubble. Søndergaard, covered with blood, staggered from the doorway and was taken to a nearby flat, and a doctor was called. Lillelund mingled with the thousands who quickly gathered to watch fireman stare stupidly at the mess.   Nothing was burning, of course, and the damage done to the Forum not only kept it from becoming a barracks but also made it unusable for the next twelve years. Lillelund heard someone say, 'Saboteurs, all right—at least twenty of them. They drove right into the Forum in a hay lorry with the bomb.'

Lillelund smiled when someone else added, 'Must have been a hell of a bomb—there's no sign of the lorry anywhere.'

The Germans had to allow the legal newspapers to report the Forum attack briefly. The explosion was not, as the saboteurs had hoped, picked up by the sensitive broadcasting microphones in the Danish State Radio studios across Rosenørns Allé, but it nevertheless resounded all over Denmark. A few days later the citizens of Esbjerg, Aalborg, and Odense, spurred by the obvious growth of the Resistance and angered by the brutal rules the Germans had been gradually imposing, confidently went on strike against the occupation forces, and on 28th August the Germans issued an ultimatum to the Danish Government that stipulated, among other things, 'Sabotage and any incitement thereto, attacks on units of the Wehrmacht or on single members thereof, possession of firearms or explosives after 1st September, 1943, shall be immediately punishable by death.'

Refusing to accept these conditions, the Danish Government resigned, and the Freedom Council stepped forward and soon established secret diplomatic links with Washington, London, and Moscow. Sabotage actions had finally frayed away the Germans' thin patience, and Danes no longer would feel obliged to apologize to the West for a Government too limp to refuse serving the Germans.

·   ·   ·   ·   ·

Late in 1941 Copenhagen's first sabotage operations took place when a small group of men filled a cigar box with a mixture of calcium chlorate and sugar, covered with wax paper. A few drops of acid, eating through the paper, detonated the powder. More cautious saboteurs later used two layers of wax paper. Unless all Copenhagen businesses that aided the Germans were sabotaged, the Danish Resistance had decided, the Allies would have to be asked to bomb the city, and the Danes wanted to prevent this. Therefore the daily thudding of explosions in Copenhagen did much for the morale of loyal Danes, although during the first days of the occupation many less anti-Nazi people there were opposed to such violent forms of resistance. Copenhagen had two major sabotage groups, BOPA and Holger Danske, working independently of one another but with the same end in view. One of the few times Holger Danske and BOPA ever took part in a joint action was when the Resistance decided to strike at the more than twenty German Army petrol dumps in Copenhagen. Dividing the dumps between the two sabotage groups, all were blown up almost at the same moment.

BOPA was formed by half-a-dozen Danish Communists, veterans of the International Brigade in Spain, who considered sabotage to be the only practical partisan warfare for flat, densely populated Denmark. A devastatingly efficient cadre, most of the original BOPA leaders were nevertheless eventually caught by the Germans. At first the group was named KOPA ('Communist Partisans'), but later when many non-Communists increased the group's membership to about 150 men, its name became BOPA ('*Borgerlige Partisaner*'— roughly, 'Middle-Class Partisans'). Because nearly all BOPA's men were either in their early twenties or younger, the group usually managed to move about unnoticed. Mostly working-class youngsters, they considered no job too difficult, and they even undertook creating a liquidation section which had the unpleasant task of destroying informers.

BOPA specialized in large-scale industrial sabotage but was not permitted to receive air-dropped explosives from Britain until late in 1944, so the group systematically looted Danish military and Wehrmacht stores for arms and explosives. Getting these materials became more and more difficult as German vigilance increased, and BOPA members decided to buy explosives through legal channels. This also proved difficult, however, because no industrial explosives were allowed to be produced in Denmark during the occupation. The men of BOPA then wrote letters to the occupation authorities claiming to need explosives for industrial demolition work in Denmark. Their letters were so convincing that the requisitions were approved by the Germans in Denmark and sent to the Reich. Once, using this scheme and claiming that material was needed to blow up a ship submerged in a channel in the Kattegat, BOPA bought 5,000 kilograms of dynamite from Germany on a single application.

Sabotage raids could not be made by unarmed men, and both Holger Danske and BOPA used weapons stolen from the German Army as well as from the Danish military, but only Holger Danske at first received the weapons dropped into Denmark by the Royal Air Force. So in 1944 BOPA chose a peculiar solution to its weapon problem. Quite a few Sten guns were then in Denmark, and Stig Jensen lent one of these to the leaders of BOPA. The gun was taken to a garage on Lyngbyvej, a main road on the northern outskirts of Copenhagen, where a blacksmith studied the weapon carefully and from it was able to produce a set of dies. Soon a clandestine production line was in operation, despite the fact that Copenhagen was patrolled thoroughly by German troops. BOPA guns were identical with Sten guns, but the sabotage group could not manufacture barrels for their weapons, so BOPA men stole rifle barrels from a Danish Army dump, and more than four hundred guns were made successfully. Later Holger Danske also produced such weapons.

BOPA then decided to try to produce naval torpedoes to launch against German shipping in Danish ports. One of the first prototypes was tested, not in Copenhagen but in the channel leading into the Funnen port of Odense, where several Resistance men sneaked to the water's edge at dusk and launched the four-foot-long, welded, boat-shaped missile. It cruised just below the surface of the water directly toward a German Navy ship. But something was wrong with the torpedo and it veered round the bows of the ship and then behind the vessel. Why did it refuse to go off? At any moment the saboteur group expected a gigantic explosion, but they heard no sound except the lap-lap of the water. Then the nose of their torpedo appeared round the stern of the German boat; and the saboteurs watched in fascination—proud of their lethal toy but puzzled by its odd behaviour.

Then: 'Run for it!'

A concussion like a sharp gust of wind reached them as the torpedo nudged the shore—at the point from which it had been launched. The men were barely out of range of the falling shrapnel.

The Holger Danske is a white stone statue of a Danish saga hero in the crypt of Elsinore castle; according to legend, he will rise in troubled times to protect Denmark. Eight politically nationalistic Danes created the first Holger Danske sabotage group, but it had to be dispersed after the Forum action. A second group with the same name was formed by Jens Lillelund and grew to about 450 men of every Danish political persuasion. Some of its men first did sabotage work for BOPA and then switched to Holger Danske because they did not like BOPA's politics. Unlike BOPA, Holger Danske was almost always able to operate in small groups, and men in each of the cells knew only their fellow workers, and then only by cover names. This reduced the chance of a security leak if any of the men were captured by the Germans. Like BOPA, this group also had a small liquidation cell; it took care of more than two hundred informers.

Most Holger Danske raids were so well planned that they seemed uninteresting, but every action meant new problems in keeping innocent people from being hurt, in escaping before the police or Germans came, and in working with limited materials. Typical was a raid on a small factory near Copenhagen's harbour, which made fuselages and wings for German training aircraft.

Ten Holger Danske men boldly stopped traffic at either end of the factory's street while three saboteurs carried bombs into the building. Holger Danske was at the time desperately short of safety fuze, and the longest delay on any of the three charges was to be only forty seconds. Jørgen Brandt, whose Bornholm accent made Copenhagen a risky centre of activities for him, carried a twenty-pound charge alone into a first-floor room, placed it on a machine, and then stacked eight one-gallon tins of inflammable paint thinner around it.

When he heard the other two saboteurs call that they were ready, Jørgen lit a fuse and rushed toward the workshop door. But the cylinder lock had closed, and the door could only be opened from the other side. Frantic, Jørgen rushed toward the window—but he did not have to jump out, for his bomb detonated and he was blown to the ground. Unwounded but smoke-blackened, his clothing tattered, Jørgen ran toward a gate. He was almost caught again when a second charge detonated and a wall collapsed just behind him.

The other saboteurs had fled, and Jørgen was alone in the blazing factory's yard. Dashing through a gate, he saw a group of Danes pushing a stalled motor-car. He began helping them, hoping the Germans he now saw coming toward the factory would not notice him.

Then, over his shoulder, Jørgen noticed one German police-constable staring hard at him. The saboteur ran, scrambled over several high walls, and finally into another factory where workers helped him wash, lent him a bicycle and fresh clothes, and hid him until he could flee.

After the first wave of sabotage in Copenhagen the German occupation authorities told the Danish police that extra vigilance was needed. How could they block the saboteurs, the police asked, without more knowledge of the places likely to be attacked? The Germans were persuaded to provide the Danish police with lists of every Danish factory likely to be sabotaged. Then the Germans were asked to give the police complete drawings showing the dispositions of guards and watchmen, and the vulnerable points in these places. Although some Danish police co-operated willingly with the Germans, from the beginning others saw to it that all Nazi security information was available to both BOPA and Holger Danske. Fire brigade, harbour, and municipal engineering offices also helped the saboteurs, so no raids were haphazard. Thus, before the Forum was attacked, Søndergaard and Lillelund went to the Frederiksberg Town Hall for complete drawings of the exhibition building.

Most sabotage raids had to be daytime operations in order to take the Germans by surprise, and because of the curfew in force after 1943. The time of the Forum raid was selected to make it heard by the greatest number of people and also to avoid hurting innocent Danes who, at any other time of the day, might have been in or near the building. Holger Danske men often disguised themselves as policemen or used forged Nazi credentials, and BOPA men frequently appeared either as members of boys' clubs or labourers.

None of the saboteurs was, in the beginning, experienced in handling explosives, and until late in the war only Holger Danske men were coached by parachutists dropped by the British.

The groups could find no place in Denmark sufficiently isolated to experiment with explosives, and new techniques always had to be tried in action. To equip the underground army that was to rise and fight during the liberation the Danes Secretly produced rockets and launchers similar to the American bazooka, but these weapons were never tried by the saboteurs. Børge Thing, leader of BOPA at the time of Denmark's liberation, did obtain a genuine American bazooka which he decided could be made to destroy German petrol tanks. Thing took the weapon out to a field next to a storage tank, put a rocket in the rear of the tube, connected its wires, then fired the projectile. But he was short of the target. He fired several more rockets but had to leave hurriedly, pursued by German guards, without scoring a direct hit.

Very late in the war, when BOPA had access to British explosives, they were given some limpet mines. One evening in March 1945 a diver in a frogman suit stolen from the Danish Navy entered Copenhagen harbour and managed to attach more than 400 pounds of mines to one German ship. These mines, however, failed to explode, and it was not until just before the end of the war that BOPA did manage to use these limpets successfully, when they penned up in Copenhagen harbour a number of large Danish ships which were to have been used to evacuate German civilians to Denmark as the Russians moved westward.

BOPA had no monopoly on unusual weapons. Many Holger Danske actions were timed so closely that the saboteurs had to retreat under gunfire. To lessen their danger they built several armoured cars, sandwiching armour plating between the doors of normal Ford V-8 saloons. In particularly dangerous operations bullet-proofing could be pulled over the rear windows, and steel curtains lowered to protect the cars' tyres.

One Holger Danske operation—although not sabotage—was so incredible that the Freedom Council envoy in Moscow received a request from Molotov for a detailed report of the action, and the Russian amused other members of the Yalta Conference during a lull with this document. The Freedom Council, suspecting that the Germans would destroy Denmark's largest, most modern ferryboat, *Storebælt*, at the end of the war, asked Holger Danske to do something about it. *Storebælt* ran between Funnen and Sealand, and in November 1944 she was to be taken around the north coast of Sealand to Copenhagen for a routine overhaul. *Storebælt*'s pilot smuggled four young Holger Danske men to a cabin in the hold. They carried 1880-model Danish service revolvers they could afford to lose, and armfuls of hand grenades they hoped they would also be able to discard. Because the voyage should have taken no more than ten hours, they carried no food.

A slow-moving German patrol boat was assigned as escort, and *Storebælt*'s crew, unaware of their four passengers, headed north. The passage up the Great Belt and into the Kattegat was rough, and that night they ran into a storm. The captain decided they must pull into Isefjord, a deep inlet in North Sealand. The saboteurs began sneaking all over the ferry, avoiding the crew, to seek food. Unable to locate the mess, they dozed in their hiding place until nearly twenty-four hours later when the pilot came to them. 'We're nearing the mouth of the Sound, just north of Elsinore.'

One of the young men ran into the engine-room, pointing his pistol down the hatch to warn: 'If the engines stop, I'm going to heave these grenades down on you!'

Another saboteur gathered the deck crew together and ordered them to do nothing.

The other two Holger Danske men went to the bridge. From there they could see the German escort ship, still quite near, and unaware anything unusual was happening on the ferry. In the distance, on a routine sweep of their waters, Swedish sailors cruised in a patrol boat. 'Full steam, hard a port! one of the saboteurs ordered *Storebælt*'s captain.

As the message was telegraphed to the engine-room the

saboteur there menacingly juggled his grenades, and the frightened Danish engineers made the ship run as quickly as they dared.

On the deck of the German patrol boat there was confusion. The Swedish patrol boat was too near the ferry for the Germans to dare shoot, and as *Storebælt* crossed into neutral waters, the Swedish ship passed between her and the Germans, finally blocking any pursuit. Not many minutes later the ferry was impounded by the Swedes, and the Holger Danske men gladly gave up their ancient weapons.

BOPA took a major rôle in preventing the total destruction of London by flying-bombs. The Globus factory outside Copenhagen was one of the four largest Danish factories producing for the Germans. For a year BOPA had wanted to destroy this radio factory, but it was as heavily guarded as a fortress, and there seemed to be no feasible way for the saboteurs to get into it. When intelligence reports showed that as well as aeroplane components Globus was making units that would be vital in a new rocket weapon, the V-2, that the Germans were planning to launch against London, BOPA began to move. The actual raid and the preparations for it took three months and, unlike commando raids on a similar scale, it could not be rehearsed but had to be executed after being planned only on paper.

Many days before the raid, teams of BOPA men dressed themselves as road workers and took tools out to the main highway that led from the Globus factory into Copenhagen. These men, working in full view of passers-by and in the daytime, set up signs indicating that the road was under repair. Neither the Danish police nor the Germans questioned the action. Then the saboteurs began tearing up the highway and digging trenches across the road-bed—in which they buried electrically wired explosive charges. Again without being bothered, they covered up the mines.

From the police, BOPA received plans of the Globus buildings and were able to draw maps showing the disposition of the German guards around the factory, which was set back several hundred yards from the main road. Late in the afternoon of 6th June, 1944, more than a hundred BOPA men assembled on the outskirts of Copenhagen with knapsacks and bicycles. They could have been a boys' camping club, but in their packs were guns, ammunition, and grenades.

The men crept into the gardens of houses near the factory and trained their weapons on any of the residents curious enough to ask what was happening. In full daylight at precisely seven o'clock in the evening they rushed forward toward the barbed-wire, firing sub-machine guns and lobbing grenades at the guards. Blasting their way through the factory gates the young saboteurs raced to the positions where they had planned to set up their mines. Having placed the explosive charges, they worked through the factory yard to the rear where, according to plan, two buses sent from Copenhagen waited.

Before the first explosives destroyed the factory the buses were lurching along the main highway. The saboteurs got clean away, and did not have to blow up the roads behind them to impede pursuers. Passing another German-controlled factory on the way toward the centre of Copenhagen the men heard the sound of gunfire. The drivers hit their accelerator pedals harder. Bullets ripped through the buses, and a young doctor driving the first one slumped over the steering-wheel. He was eased to the floor and someone else climbed behind the wheel. Both buses reached Copenhagen where the group dispersed, with the doctor, whose wounds proved fatal, as the only casualty of the expedition. This, the first really big daylight sabotage attack in Denmark, so successfully impeded V-2 production that it earned a radioed message of congratulations from General Eisenhower's SHAEF headquarters.

.   .   .   .   .

In the following months BOPA attacked all the other Copenhagen factories producing V-2 components, and every raid was a success. One of these factories was on a peninsula south of Copenhagen, and it was impossible to surround it, so BOPA decided on a frontal attack. In two lorries they sent men to the factory with a pair of 20-mm. field guns stolen from a Danish Army depot. At the factory entrance the guns were wheeled from their lorries and began to fire rapidly, demolishing the guard posts. Firing sub-machine guns from the hip, the raiders charged into the factory. Both the Danish and German guards answered the gunfire, and fighting continued while the saboteurs lugged their explosives into position and lit the fuses. In a fighting retreat the saboteurs had to leave their artillery behind, but the action was a success; the factory was razed as completely as it would have been if it had been hit by bombers.

Between 1942 and 1945 BOPA and Holger Danske each staged more than a thousand separate actions, thus sparing wholesale Allied bombardment of Copenhagen.

5

According to Plan

TORBEN ØRUM was a man worth watching. When the Germans came, Ørum, thirty-nine years old and the Danish Air Force's youngest lieutenant-colonel, set up a private espionage network. His agents, young lieutenants demobilized by the Danish Army in 1940, worked as labourers near German camps and airfields to spy on the occupation forces. Eventually, Ørum hoped, his men could escape westward, either to be trained as agents to be returned to Denmark or to fight in uniform alongside the British. Colonel Ørum, not a trained intelligence officer, was indeed a man worth watching—which unfortunately the Germans did very closely.

When Ørum went to Sweden to relay information to the British Legation in Stockholm, he made the mistake of travelling on an ordinary visa, and German agents followed him. Back in Denmark, advised by officer friends that he was about to be arrested, Ørum and one of his officers, Lieutenant Jessen, daringly caught a train for Germany, hoping to be able to make their way through France and Spain to England. But the tall, aristocratic-looking colonel was an easy man to keep in sight, and he and Jessen were arrested before they got as far as France.

Still making a show of allowing Denmark to appear self-governing, the Germans returned both officers to Copenhagen for trial. It would be wise, German authorities suggested to the Danish courts, to condemn the pair to death. Since Denmark had no capital punishment, and no Danish laws existed to deal with such cases harshly enough to please the Germans, a special 'Lex Ørum' was enacted to avoid a German-imposed death penalty. The Colonel received a twelve-year prison sentence, and Jessen was sentenced to ten years.

Ørum was in a Danish prison in 1943 after the Danish Government resigned, and the Germans decided to reopen his case. A Resistance group, learning that Ørum was to be taken to the Reich to be executed, began a most unusual military action—in the stockroom of a bookshop on the ground floor of the Nazi headquarters building in Copenhagen's Town Hall Square.

Mogens Staffeldt's bookshop in Dagmarhus was a crossroads of Resistance activity. Whenever Resistance members could not convene safely there for daily meetings, Staffeldt sign-posted a warning with certain combinations of books placed in one of his display windows. A small, quiet man, then in his late twenties, Staffeldt knew how to contact any category of Resistance people. Through Colonel Ørum's wife he learned that Ørum was ill in the Copenhagen Military Hospital in Tagensvej, a boulevard near the centre of the city, and he passed this information to Major Svend Truelsen, a young barrister, who, as an officer in the Royal Life Guard, then led the Danish Army and Navy underground espionage network which was in contact with the British. Mrs. Ørum helped Staffeldt arrange a meeting between Ørum's nurse, Helga von Seck, and Truelsen.

Miss von Seck, a Danish Army nursing sister, described to Truelsen the hospital's security arrangements and also the pair of Danish police guards brought from a local civilian prison to watch over Ørum. Working in two shifts, one of the policemen always kept the colonel in sight. 'They're terrified of him,' she said. 'He promised never to try to escape when their backs are turned—but he said he might try to get away while they're watching him.'

'Would those guards help us?' Truelsen asked.

'And get sent to a concentration camp? No, sir! They let

the Colonel have a wireless receiver and books—which he isn't suppose to have—but that's all they'll do.'

'Assuming I could get into the hospital, could you arrange things so I can see Colonel Ørum alone?' Truelsen asked.

The nurse thought for a moment. 'Well—there's an X-ray room next to his, and it would be normal for me to ask the guard to send him in there. You'll need keys for the corridor and for that room—' She grinned. 'But that's easy. Easier than getting past the German military guards at the hospital entrance.'

Miss von Seck promised to steal the two hospital keys for Truelsen, and they arranged a meeting in the X-ray room.

The four main buildings of the Copenhagen Military Hospital formed a large quadrangle which could be entered only through a fifteen-feet-wide arched passageway through the administration building that fronted on Tagensvej. Truelsen arrived at the hospital clad in a white cotton surgical coat, and none of the German military policemen tried to stop him as he walked past their guardroom at the left of the entrance, through the tunnel-like archway, and into the quadrangle. Truelsen noticed that hospital patients occasionally strolled between the ranks of trees or sat on the benches that lined the concrete walks of the courtyard. Not pausing, the young major walked straight to the far end of the high, tiled-roofed building that faced from the quadrangle's right. He went into the doorway at the end of the building, up a few steps, and let himself into the X-ray room at the left of the entrance-way to the long corridor.

'Here's the Colonel for his X-rays, Doctor,' Miss von Seck announced a few minutes later, ushering Ørum into the small room where Truelsen waited. The Danish police guard peered into the room, then withdrew and locked the door. Quietly the major and the colonel discussed the situation. Escape seemed impossible, Ørum stated flatly. The high wooden fence around the hospital was patrolled at all times by German guards. The only way out of the compound was the tunnel through the administration building to Tagensvej, and a squad of German military policemen always sat in the guardroom. At night all the guards were especially alert, and in the day-time Germans were all over the hospital. But escape would, Truelsen insisted, be possible, and he began outlining the tactics of the plan.

Leaving the hospital that evening Truelsen noticed that, as Ørum had said, Germans seemed to be everywhere, peering from the windows of the four tall buildings or slouching on the benches in the courtyard. Off to the left side of the hospital grounds lay rows of barracks full of sick Wehrmacht personnel probably not too sick to be unable to pursue a Danish fugitive. According to both the Colonel and Miss von Seck, Ørum was the best-known, most recognizable patient in the hospital.

When Truelsen strolled out through the archway the Germans merely nodded good-byes. Well, he would have no trouble getting other Resistance men into the hospital quadrangle to help him if it were properly planned. But how to get the notorious Ørum out?

A few days later, Miss von Seck arranged another meeting in the X-ray room, and Truelsen presented a finalized, detailed plan to the senior officer. It would have to be timed precisely, because if anything untoward happened the entire plan would collapse. If the plan failed, Truelsen said, there would be a lot of dead Germans, not to mention quite a few dead Danes. Ørum was pessimistic and asked if his rescue was worth such a risk. Truelsen said it certainly was, because in addition to saving a single Danish officer, it meant preventing the German intimidation of the entire Danish officer corps. Colonel Ørum would be rescued on 21st October, 1943.

At two o'clock on the afternoon of the 21st Truelsen marshalled all the Life Guard reserve officers in the operation at the offices of the Danish Agricultural Council. One of the only civilians in the meeting, Jens Lillelund, had been invited because Truelsen admired his coolness and because Lillelund's Holger Danske saboteurs would later on have a hand in the action. All of the men wore normal civilian clothing except Truelsen, Lillelund and two of the officers, who had white hospital coats. Every one of the men at the meeting had either a sub-machine gun or a pistol. In mid-afternoon, their briefing complete, they set out in taxis.

Bicycles glided up and down Tagensvej past the hospital when the first two taxis drew up. One stationed itself opposite the German sentry post at the left-hind corner of the Military Hospital compound facing Tagensvej; the other covered the right-hand sentry, in order to attack the German military police if something went wrong inside the hospital. A third taxi arrived, parked directly across the street from the hospital entrance, and Truelsen stepped out with Lillelund and two of the other white-coated officers. All three wore glasses. A fourth officer, dressed in civilian clothes, remained in the taxi until he saw the first three walk into the hospital entrance, past the guards and through the arcade. Then this last officer, Captain Lunn, a husky man well over six feet tall, also began to stroll toward the entrance-way.

Earlier that afternoon Colonel Ørum had been to the hospital massage clinic, and when he returned to his room he asked to be allowed to be taken for a walk in the compound. Helga von Seck arranged permission for the Colonel to be in the yard between four-thirty and five in the afternoon.

As three of the men walked toward the rear of the building in which Ørum was kept, Captain Lunn boldly went into the German guardroom and asked to see a doctor. The physician's name was one that Truelsen's men had selected after a careful check to see that there was no such doctor in the hospital. Truelsen, Lillelund, and the third man, Lieutenant Skeel, walked awkwardly because they were carrying a number of things.

Skeel was the most stiff, because under his white coat he held a sub-machine gun. The fourth officer, Lieutenant Scavenius, paused inside the compound, just to the left of the entrance. He stood idly, his coat also concealing a sub-machine gun.

Skeel halted a few feet outside the doorway to cover Lillelund and Truelsen when they entered the building in which Ørum was kept. The two men paused in the tiny vestibule opposite the X-ray room, and Lieutenant Scavenius came in just behind them. A few minutes later Colonel Ørum and his guard emerged from the Colonel's bedroom fifteen feet away. The Colonel was wearing his overcoat over civilian clothes and was ready for his walk in the yard. As they passed into the vestibule Lillelund stepped from behind a doorway and clapped a hand over the Danish guard's mouth. At the same moment Truelsen jabbed a pistol in the guard's stomach. Scavenius was just behind the other two, and he and Lillelund forced the man into the X-ray room, and Colonel Ørum and Truelsen followed, locking the door behind them.

'Keep quiet or we'll kill you,' Lillelund ordered, taking his hand from the guard's mouth.

The policeman looked pleadingly at Truelsen. 'W-w-won't you please put down your pistol? Maybe we can talk this over.'

'I never put down my pistol when it's pointed at a man's stomach,' Truelsen replied.

'This is going to get me in trouble—in terrible trouble !' the guard protested.

'If you have any troubles,' Lillelund snapped, 'get in touch with us. We'll have you sent to Sweden.'

As Lillelund ordered the guard to empty his pockets, Truelsen handed the Colonel a pair of thick-framed glasses, a handkerchief, and a hat Mrs. Ørum had provided. Pocketing the guard's identity papers—they might come in handy later—Lillelund Scavenius began to bind the man up, atop a mattress they had dragged to the floor. Before they were finished,

Truelsen and Colonel Ørum were outside the small room and stepping out toward the door.

A customs cruiser was docking at that moment in a harbour in Copenhagen, and the two Danish Navy officers who had stolen the boat with the help of the Sound customs officer, now waited, occasionally checking their wrist-watches. They nodded affably at the Gestapo guard on the quay, then wondered if he would cause trouble later. Both Danes wore borrowed customs uniforms.

Ørum and Truelsen walked out past Skeel without a sign, then turned right and began strolling toward the opposite side of the courtyard. Several hospital patients idly glanced at them. Germans peered from the windows, but Miss von Seck had passed word around that the Danish Colonel was going to be allowed to take a little therapeutic exercise in the compound. The two officers turned left, then reached the end of the walk at the far side of the compound and turned left again.

In the X-ray room Lillelund and Scavenius used bandages to bind the policeman as tightly as a mummy, and Lillelund forced a rifle cartridge into the guard's mouth, warning him that if he tried to yell, he would swallow it. Adhesive tape sealed the guard's lips. Skeel remained alertly on guard behind the building. Colonel Ørum nervously held a handkerchief, ready to pretend to blow his nose. Now the problem was to get past the guardroom. It was all a scene from pantomime, only the usual scuffling sounds of daily routine breaking the silence.

As Colonel Ørum and Major Truelsen approached the arcade Captain Lunn was still in the guardroom talking to a German who was leafing through the hospital directory. Lunn had orders to try to shoot all the Germans if they as much as noticed Ørum. Through the small window Lunn saw Ørum approach. Then the tall captain, according to plan, began fumbling with his hands and suddenly spilled the contents of a small white box. Medicinal capsules began rolling over the floor of the guardroom. 'Oh, damn it!' Lunn said.

All the men in the guardroom began scrambling around on the floor, retrieving the pills that rolled under the desks and tables, into every corner. Lunn watched the guards, his hands now tensely gripping the machine pistol under his coat.

Not one of the Germans was looking through the guard-room window when Ørum and Truelsen walked past, left the entrance and strode across Tagensvej to the waiting taxi. The back door of the cab was opened, and its engine was running. An army officer in civilian clothes sat next to the driver.

In the guardroom Lunn thanked the Germans politely for picking up the capsules which he then counted carefully. 'My colleague must be working in one of the other hospitals in Tagensvej today,' he explained apologetically, and left.

Lillelund and Scavenius now had bound the guard tightly. They tossed a packet of British cigarettes—these had been in a parachuted container—on the floor. Then they calmly walked from the X-ray room, carefully locking the door behind them.

Skeel, seeing Lillelund and Scavenius come outside, also began walking toward the hospital exit. The Germans merely nodded at all of the Resistance men, doubtless thinking they were on the hospital staff.

Truelsen's taxi had already gone, and when the other men reached the street, the taxis covering the sentry posts also moved off.

Ørum sat nervously in the taxi with Truelsen. 'They'll be certain to follow us,' he said.

'Nonsense, sir,' Truelsen smiled. 'They probably don't even know you've gone. Anyway, we're rather well covered.'

Truelsen ordered the chauffeur to drive to Trianglen. The young officer looked through the rear window of the taxi but saw no cars apparently following them. Their taxi had turned left at the roundabout into Blegdamsvej, had passed the Niels Bohr Institute, and was heading north-west toward Trianglen, a busy traffic intersection. There the driver stopped and Truelsen paid him. When the car had driven off Truelsen led Ørum toward another taxi that had been engaged by an officer and was waiting on schedule. They climbed inside and found a peaked cap with a badge on the front of it reading 'Customs Inspector'. 'Here, sir,' Truelsen told the Colonel, 'put this on. It's your size.'

Back at the hospital, Helga von Seck went about her business, careful to avoid Colonel Ørum's room. The police guard, still bound and gagged in the X-ray room, struggled, trying to reach the telephone on the window-sill.

Truelsen's taxi went to Bergensgade and was changed for a third cab which cruised through the Hellerup suburb toward Tuborg Harbour where the Sound customs cruiser was waiting by the quay on which the Gestapo man still stood. The taxi drew up and Colonel Ørum, now more calm and carrying a pistol Truelsen had given him, stepped out. Ørum began to say good-bye, but Truelsen gestured him to continue to board the cruiser. 'I can never thank you enough,' Ørum said. 'You saved my life.'

'It was only my duty,' replied Truelsen.

When the two officers came abreast of the Gestapo man he looked at Ørum and nodded. The Colonel glanced at the German, said, 'Good evening', and walked with Truelsen to the cruiser. As Ørum stepped aboard the customs boat wearing the cap, the two men on deck saluted and smiled. Truelsen walked to the end of the long pier to watch the boat safely away.

It was five-thirty in the evening—dusk—when they drew away from the quay under the eyes of the Gestapo man, headed out into the harbour, their lights lit and the flag of the Danish customs authority flying, and then cruised northward along the Danish coast of the Sound. Abreast of Charlottenlund the small boat veered eastward, put out its lights, and the noise of its strong engines rose as it raced across the water. Less thin two hours later it reached its destination in Sweden and the only remaining problem was returning it to where it belonged—a task which Holger Danske would facilitate. Setting off two sabotage charges at a pair of German factory buildings at nine o'clock that night Holger Danske successfully diverted all the German units along the Sound away from the small quay. The boat was returned safely.

Later that evening Truelsen gathered together for a celebration party about ten of the men who had helped free the Colonel. Nobody had been captured. Before the party was too far under way Truelsen telephoned the Danish Military Hospital and asked to speak to one of the German authorities. 'If you unlock your X-ray room,' Truelsen said, 'you'll find a guard tied up there.'

There was a pause. Truelsen heard mumbling on the other end of the line, then a voice asked him, 'Would you wait a minute, please?'

'We never wait,' Truelsen said, hanging up the telephone.

The guard in the X-ray room had, in fact, much earlier been able to knock the telephone off the window-sill, and he had been freed. When the Germans had then called in Helga von Seck to describe what clothes the Colonel wore that day, she withheld nothing. She had no reason to lie, because an hour before she had had a telephone call from Major Truelsen saying that Ørum was safely in Sweden.

6
'J.J. Has been Caught'

WHEN Arne Sejr lived in a furnished room in central Copenhagen in 1942 his identification card said he was a student, but directing the students' Resistance movement left him little time for classes.

Two o'clock one morning in December 1942 bad news was brought to Arne's room. A pair of young men carrying valises into the building earlier that night had been seen by a police patrol who, thinking the two youths might have been burglars, opened the luggage—and found bundles of illegal newspapers. Warned about this, Sejr kept a careful watch at his darkened window, and when later he saw the blue lights of a police car pull up to the kerb outside, he took a suitcase he had already packed, slipped down the stairs and out into the back yard. The remaining hours of that night he slept in the flat of student friends, and from then until the end of the occupation he had to remain underground.

Partly because the Germans cleverly maintained Danish legal jurisdiction during the occupation's first years, and partly because Danes habitually obey laws, few Resistance people went underground until they had to. During his first fugitive months Arne Sejr wanted to turn and run whenever he saw policemen or German soldiers, although he knew that anonymous detectives or civilian informers were more likely to trap him. He realized, moreover, that any attempt he might make to disguise himself would only attract attention, for Copenhagen is an affable city where one frequently meets one's acquaintances.

56

The underground's incredible machinery provided Arne with a new identity. With cards stolen from police desks and with rubber stamps either procured the same way or carefully forged, Arne's friends manufactured his new credentials. His cover name was entered into the Danish Folk Registry, a list of everyone resident in Denmark. If captured, his papers would be checked, so he was given a bogus birth record. Seven Jutland villages have the same name, and this name was often used as the birthplace on forged credentials, since the Nazis were usually too lazy to check into seven different files of birth records. Danish clergymen could be counted on to enter such false births in their parish records.

Arne's papers said he was a student because that was a convenient occupation to allow freedom of movement, and his cover name was enrolled in one of the Copenhagen colleges where his bursar's fee was paid. Whenever he maintained a permanent address, he had to be careful to keep the hours a student would keep; and when he returned home late, he pretended to have been at a party. He dared keep nothing incriminating in his rented rooms. Carefully composed letters were mailed to him under his new name, and he usually carried these to substantiate his identity.

A considerable part of every day was spent trying to find a place to sleep at night. He sometimes curled up near central heating furnaces in large office buildings, or in the basements of bakers' shops. When forced to stay in hotels, he chose the types used for other sorts of clandestine meetings, and to appear unobtrusive he would book a double room, then quit it early in the morning. Hiding him made other people parties to what were said to be his crimes, but all sorts of people sheltered him. He might sleep in a villa in the palatial Hellerup suburb one might and in a slum tenement the next. In all, he lived in nearly a hundred places in Copenhagen illegally, and because he did not have a place to sleep on 27th September, 1943, he suffered one of his worst experiences of the occupation.

That evening Sejr and Niels Thymer Larsen, another young member of the students' group, had climbed the lift-shaft in a naval warehouse on Copenhagen's island of Amager to steal some old Danish Navy pistols that had been overlooked by the Germans when they confiscated all Danish military weapons a month earlier. Most of the pistols the boys carried down the lift-shaft were 1910 models that lacked firing pins, so they took the weapons directly to their gun shop and arsenal, a rented room round the corner from the Copenhagen Town Hall. They reached the second-floor room at 10 Mikkel Bryggers-gade at nine o'clock, an hour after curfew, and rather than risk being caught on the street with identity papers that would not withstand close scrutiny, they decided to spend the night there.

Not yet tired enough to sleep, the boys took a typewriter from under the bed and began pecking out, on a mimeograph stencil, the text for *Studenternes Efterretningstjenste*. When they heard footsteps on the stairs at about half-past nine, they hastily hid the typewriter. There was a knock at the door, and Arne opened it to a pair of Danish policemen.

The police peered around at the shabby, ill-matched tables and chairs, at the old bed, and at the two large cupboards, one blocking the door that swung open into the adjoining flat. This furniture was conspicuously poor for a well-kept building, but it was all the students had been able to afford.

'Boys, we can see slits of light from your windows. Your blackout curtains aren't tight.'

Niels and Arne glanced at the three windows facing on Mikkel Bryggersgade. 'The curtains looked all right to me,' Sejr replied, 'but we'll fix them.'

When the policemen left the boys found that the curtains had not been leaking light. 'Arne, should we go out and try to find somewhere else to sleep tonight? You know, there's a Danish Nazi living downstairs—' Niel's voice broke off.

'It would look pretty suspicious if we left now,' Sejr replied. They decided to remain in the room, but as a precaution they removed only their shoes before flicking off the light and sprawling on the bed at about eleven o'clock.

Some instinct wakened them both at about one in the morning, and they heard a motor-car stop outside. As heavy footsteps clomped up the stairs Arne whispered, 'Come on! Let's move!'

In the darkness they tugged on their shoes, then quickly slid the second cupboard full of weapons against the door that opened out on to the landing. Each of them pocketed a pistol and some ammunition, and they tiptoed to the left-hand window as the doorbell rang in the adjoining flat. Muffled German voices came from the stairs.

As in many old Copenhagen buildings, the large panes of glass in the three windows were fixed permanently in place, but above each large window were pairs of smaller windows that swung outward horizontally. On the next floor above was another flat, and over it was the roof, its eaves projecting about two feet. Arne and Niels decided they could climb up the front of the building and escape over the rooftops. Except for narrow cement window-sills jutting outward only a few inches, the painted plaster exterior wall could hardly have been smoother if it had been polished.

They climbed through the window and stood on the sill. The street below was dark and empty of people. There was at least a thirty-foot drop to the pavement. Niels, using the smaller windows' frame as a ladder, began climbing, but could not reach as high as the window-sill on the next floor. Arne, clinging to the building with one hand, pushed Niels upward with his other. From inside they heard the German policemen clubbing the barricaded door.

Niels groped upward on the smooth wall, but still he could not reach high enough. 'Give me a shove!' he whispered.

Raising his right hand high, Arne found the gritty heel on Niels' shoe, then forced it hard upward. At the same moment Niels tried to leap. 'I've got the sill,' he called down, 'but I can't get to the window to smash it.'

'Take my pistol and try to get at the window with the butt.'

Dangling by one arm, Niels reached down for the pistol.

Through the window Arne saw the cupboard sway each time the cursing Germans hurled their shoulders against the blocked door. 'Hurry up, Niels! They'll be in the room in a minute! I'll have to move or they'll see me !'

Arne hugged the building face and reached his left leg across until he felt the edge of the next window's sill with his toe. Now he was spread-eagled between the two windows, his cheek flat against the wall. If he could remain there, the Germans would not see him unless they broke the large pane and poked their heads out. Arne wondered how long he could hold on, and he pressed his body flatly against the building as hard as he could.

'Arne,' Niels whispered; 'see if you can give me another boost.'

Arne shoved again at Niels' foot. Again Niels leaped. Then above Arne heard a crash of glass and a woman's scream.

'Shut up, you damned fool!' Niels hissed. Then to Arne:

'Here—take back your pistol. I'm climbing inside to see if there's something I can use to pull you up.'

Just then there was a crash as the cupboard fell forward and the door to the landing opened.

'There!' one of the Germans yelled, pointing at one of Niels' feet that still dangled just below the top of the window. The German fired his pistol but missed the foot. Niels pulled himself into the third-floor flat as the Germans began breaking the large glass pane out of the second-floor window.

'Can you see them outside?' one of them ordered. Arne saw a hand holding a pistol reach cautiously out of the window next to him.

'Oh, go on!' the voice snapped. 'Have a look outside!'

'And get shot? Not on your life !' was the reply.

Arne's fingers were getting cold and numb when he heard one of the Germans say, 'Let's go upstairs and head them off!'

As soon as Arne heard the door close he climbed gingerly back into the room, and trying to make no noise, crunched through the broken glass to get across the room to the door that connected with the other flat. He would never be able to sneak down the tight, angular staircase without being heard, but there might be a way through from the room beyond.

Niels, meanwhile, had convinced the woman he had awakened that she should be silent, but he found nothing to lower as a rope, and decided to get away to the roof.

Remembering which way the connecting door swung into the room, Arne grabbed the left end of the cupboard and began to pivot it out of the way. He would have to reach for the doorknob with his right hand and to hold his pistol in his left. He was a poor shot with his left hand, but he could only approach the door from its left.

Cautiously he drew back the door. Facing him was a Gestapo man pointing a pistol. As he pulled the trigger of his own weapon, Arne saw the Gestapo man's pistol flash. Something pinched at Arne's thigh. His own pistol merely clicked—a misfire.

He toppled to the floor, and two men pounced on him. Blood from the wound in his leg seeped through his trousers, but the bullet had passed cleanly through the flesh. His wound did not hurt, but he sensed that he must pretend to be crippled.

Niels was now on the roof, and when one of the Germans went to the top of the building to lean out of an attic window, the boy took a pot-shot at him with his pistol.

The two Gestapo men finally pushed Arne against the wall where he stood heron-fashion on his left leg, wincing in pretended agony. He answered none of their questions.

'You've got three minutes,' one of the Germans ordered, eyeing his wrist-watch and pointing a pistol at Arne, 'and if you haven't begun talking, I'll shoot you.' He began reading off the seconds. If he shoots me, Arne thought, he won't learn a thing.

When the three minutes had passed, the Gestapo man lowered his pistol and ordered Arne to take down his trousers so they could see his wound.

Another motor-car pulled into Mikkel Bryggersgade, and Niels' pistol barked several times from the roof. Arne heard footsteps on the stairs and two burly policemen from the Copenhagen riot squad entered the wrecked room. The Germans searching through the two cupboards had found about seventy-five pistols, and even the Danish policemen were impressed, because to be caught with just one pistol meant a death sentence. The fatter of the Gestapo men held his ear to the fallen cupboard. 'Something's ticking in there !'

The German pulled out the unarmed mechanism of a boobytrap clock, and Arne tried not to smile as the terrified man rushed to throw the harmless clock down the stair well, smashing it on the stone floor several storeys below.

Arne continued to pretend to be crippled when the two big Danish policemen helped him down the narrow stairs. One of the policemen whispered, 'Is there anything we can do?'

'Just tell people J. J. has been caught,' Arne answered. 'J. J.' was then his Resistance name.

Other Danish police who came to set up searchlights in Mikkel Bryggersgade to trap Niels were purposefully clumsy. But they blocked off the building on one side of number ten, and the other adjacent roof was too high for Niels' escape. He could only perch near the chimney to snipe from behind it at anyone who dared approach him.

The German police who drove Arne across Copenhagen questioned him continually. 'What is your name?' 'Are you a Communist?' 'What political party do you belong to?' All the way to the hospital in Nyelandsvej in Frederiksberg, Arne said nothing.

A doctor and a policeman, both in German uniforms, questioned him in the hospital. He would not answer, and the more they threatened him with pistols, the more stubborn he became. The doctor, after making Arne remove his trousers, snapped, 'You're faking, boy. That wound isn't so bad!'

'I tell you, it hurts!' Arne cried.

Grimly the doctor bandaged the bullet holes—one in the front and one in the back of the thigh—with crêpe paper bandages. German guards then dragged him through the hospital grounds toward another building. The doctor, snicking at him from behind with a riding crop, shouted, 'Walk on that leg, boy!'

'I can't!"

'Damn it, if you don't walk on it, you'll get a dangerous blood clot!"

In the next building the doctor began questioning Arne again, slashing at him more and more furiously with the riding crop. 'Answer our questions!'

Arne's face was set. The more the riding crop cut him, the more determinedly he refused to reply. The Germans worked themselves into a frenzy, and eventually Arne felt weak and dizzy. Still he said nothing—and then he fainted.

From the floor, through a crimson haze, he saw a huge policeman waving a pistol over him. The man's face was scowling, and he seemed to be mouthing words, but Arne at first heard nothing. Then he focused on the words—more questions he would not answer.

The policeman dragged him to a basement, put him in a crude cell that had been fashioned from a coal bunker, and took away all his clothes and the wrist-watch his parents had given him. After throwing him a blanket about three feet long, the Germans left. Probably they would spy on him through the small peep-hole in the door, Arne decided, so he determined to continue his act. It was not entirely an act, however, for the cell was chilly and his recent bronchitis seemed to be coming back. Arne's skin was clammy with perspiration, and his face felt red hot.

When Niels finally had used all his ammunition, the Germans

moved up to the roof to catch him. Taken to Dagmarhus, he refused to answer questions, and he was transferred to Vester Prison, then to a second prison in Copenhagen. Later he was placed in a concentration camp in Denmark for a time, and finally moved to a camp in Germany until the capitulation.

The German guards who fetched Arne in the morning tossed him only his trousers, shoes and sweater. The Nazi doctor and four Gestapo men, one an interpreter and one a clerk with a typewriter, awaited him in an examination room on the first floor of the hospital. The fattest of the Gestapo men asked questions and the typist began taking notes. Arne pretended he could not understand German and the interpreter had to repeat the questions, giving him time to make up his answers carefully. Stalling this way, Arne had time to look around the room. 'It's stuffy in here,' he finally whimpered, and one of the Germans opened a window.

They asked him about the room in Mikkel Bryggersgade, about the seventy-five guns, about Niels. Through the hospital window Arne saw German soldiers in convalescent uniforms loitering below. Beyond them was a high brick wall, and on the other side was the Danish section of the hospital. All five of the Germans with him were armed, even the doctor, and there seemed to be no escape. If only he could get out of the window . . .

More questions and more threats, and Arne knew that soon the questioners would lose patience and begin beating him again. He knew he would be forced to tell them something, so he gave the names of six Resistance people—all men he knew had been smuggled safely to Sweden.

As the typist continued to take notes, Arne glanced from time to time out of the window. He hopped around on his left foot, wincing whenever he lowered the wounded leg to the floor. His face was still flushed, and it was easy to pretend to be in pain.

Finally the typist jerked the sheets of paper from his machine, glanced at them, and passed them on to one of the Gestapo men who snapped at Arne, 'Read this and sign it!'

He should have read the paper carefully, Arne knew, but it did not seem to matter; they would do what they wanted with him. Seventy-five pistols. . . .

Some of the Germans left the room, and another came into it. Arne found himself with just two medical orderlies and the doctor, but all three had pistols. 'Your leg isn't as bad as you say, but we're going to dress it for you again, anyway,' the doctor glared, turning to a table on which were fresh paper bandages and a bottle of antiseptic. It was Arne's moment.

He turned, took two quick steps and leapt out of the window, landing amid ten Germans. He was running almost before his feet touched the ground, and the dazed soldiers stared dumbfounded as he neared the wall. 'You men, stop him! Catch that man!' the doctor screamed frantically out of the window, forgetting to use his pistol.

Arne grabbed for the top of the seven-foot wall and pulled himself up. He tore his hands on the rough bricks, and the strands of barbed wire atop the wall clawed and caught at his skin. But he got over.

The Germans all tried at once to follow him over the wall— and merely got in each others' way. Arne ran through the Danish section of the hospital and out into the street where he saw a man with a bicycle. 'Lend me your bike! Please, hurry—'

But the man stared, shook his head, and pedalled slowly away.

There seemed few people about as Arne ran down one narrow street after another. Behind him were the Germans, but he was running more quickly than they, and eventually he found himself out of their sight for a moment. Through the hallway of a block of flats he ran, then up the stairs, two at a time. On the third landing was an open door, and he rushed through it. An old lady in the room screamed, and two big men moving a piano into a corner looked up and said sternly, 'You shouldn't scare the lady like that!'

Not hesitating to argue, Arne ran through the flat and found a kitchen door that led to the back stairs. Quickly he ran down. Nobody was chasing him.

More side streets, alleys, garden walls, until he simply could go no farther. He felt as if he would burst. The Germans seemed to have lost him.

'You must help me!' he gasped, entering a small dairy shop. 'I have a weak heart, and I've had an attack!'

The woman assistant came from behind the counter and eased him into a chair. 'Can I use your phone?'

The woman nodded.

As he asked the operator for a number the woman in the shop stared at him, terrified. 'Hello,' Arne spoke into the telephone. 'Erik?' The woman's face was white, and Arne glanced down. Blood oozed from his tattered trousers; the bandage on his thigh had slipped.

The woman became even more startled as Arne told his friend, '. . . and have the taxi cruise up and down this street slowly with the back door, open. And watch out for Germans. *And* bring a pistol for me.'

When Arne hung up, the woman lent him a white overall, and he went out into the street, a bottle of milk in one hand, a loaf of bread in the other—a sweaty, limping milkman.

The taxi with his friend Erik Bunch-Christensen in the back seat cruised slowly into the road. The vehicle came abreast of Arne, he leapt in, and was driven quickly away—to a place where he could sleep again in safety.

7

Exodus

ONE afternoon in 1935 Julius Margolinsky's bookshop in Copenhagen was visited by a German-speaking man. Could he have a look at the Emil Ludwig book on Nazi concentration camps? Yes, of course he could. Did the book-seller have any more such material? No, he did not. By coincidence, the same day Margolinsky had written a polite letter declining an invitation to a Paris conference on the persecution of Spanish Loyalist youths; the pamphlet advertising the conference was still on his desk when the customer was in the shop.

Margolinsky forgot both of these things until five o'clock one morning in 1942 when German criminal policemen took him from his home to Copenhagen's Vester Prison for interrogation. Was he a Communist? No. If he was not Communist, why had he been so interested in Spanish youths back in 1935? Mr. Margolinsky tried to explain. Only after seventeen days of almost continuous questioning was he allowed to go home, and he was not bothered again by the Germans until the following year when they decided the time had come to arrest all Danish Jews.

At the start of the occupation, Denmark's sole synagogue of any noticeable size, in Copenhagen, was attended every week by no more than three or four hundred people; and of slightly less than 8,000 Jews in Denmark, nearly 1,500 were half-Jewish and about 1,400 were young refugees from Nazi Germany who worked as farm labourers on Sealand. Until the autumn of 1943, most Danes were unaware of this miniscule Jewish community.

Nazi hoodlums had tried unsuccessfully to burn the Copenhagen synagogue in 1941, but this was almost the only open Nazi act of anti-Semitism in Denmark before October 1943. On the 29th August, when the Government fell, the synagogue had been closed by the congregation's elders, but Rabbi Melchior opened it again himself. Because of Denmark's lack of racial prejudice, the Jews in the country considered themselves safe, and practically none tried to get to Sweden until the fatal autumn of 1943.

On 28th September, 1943, Attaché Duckwitz, a German maritime shipping expert in the Reich embassy in Copenhagen, warned Hans Hedtoft of the Danish Socialist Party that Denmark's Jews were about to be arrested by the Gestapo and deported to the Theresienstadt Concentration Camp in the Reich on 1st October. The Gestapo apparently had been working steadily since the beginning of the occupation, checking telephone books and other directories to determine exactly which Danes were Jews. This was quite a task because the last official list of Jews in Denmark had been compiled in 1920, and even the Jewish Community Centre in Copenhagen did not have an up-to-date mailing list—although the list they did have was confiscated by the Germans.

Who exactly, Danes now wondered, were the Jews in Denmark? How to find them? Most important, how to keep them out of the Germans' grasp? In the synagogue at the end of the Rosh Hashanah service on 29th September the congregation was advised to go into hiding. Some of these people thought this warning absurd, but most took the rabbi's advice and moved out of the city to hide in villages or on the farms of friends.

On 1st October, just as Duckwitz had said, the Gestapo order for the Jews' arrest was given, and that same night the Germans temporarily switched off Copenhagen's telephone service, frustrating last-minute attempts by Danes to warn their Jewish friends. Gestapo men raced all over Copenhagen to every Jewish home.

That day, in every hospital in the city, registers were carefully checked by staff doctors, and all patients with Jewish-sounding names were discharged, then readmitted under false names. A family of perfectly healthy Jews went to the 1,200-bed hospital in Copenhagen's Bispebjerg suburb where they were registered as patients and given beds. Another Jewish family that came to the hospital were hidden that night in a cellar. Dr. K. H. Køster, a junior surgeon of Bispebjerg's staff, began to wonder if he could help these and other Jews out of Denmark.

Mogens Staffeldt's bookshop, having been evicted from Dagmarhus when the Germans took over the building, was now opposite the Nazi-occupied Hotel d'Angleterre on the large square, Kongens Nytorv. During the first week in October the shop ceased selling books as Staffeldt used his Resistance contacts to get many of his Jewish friends transport to Sweden. Soon the shop resembled a harried travel agency as more and more Jews learned that it was a gateway to safety, but the Germans across Kongens Nytorv never noticed the activity.

A group of university people in the north-west suburb of Lyngby began carrying small boats overland from Lyngby Lake to the Sound to row Jews across to Sweden. A few Jewish families were able to persuade fishermen to carry them across the Sound, but most of these people had to pay out-landishly high fares; a fisherman would lose his boat and probably his life if caught helping such people. During the first days of October some Jewish families paid as much as 50,000 kroner for their escape.

Arne Sejr, living in a small villa in South Sealand while he recovered from his wound, soon made his hiding place into a transit centre for the young Jewish refugees who were farm workers and whom the Student's Resistance cells would get across to Sweden on secret scheduled transports they operated. Sejr's helpers in the Students' Enlightenment Service were at that time hurriedly combing all the rest of Sealand for hidden Jews to rescue.

During the first five days in October, Dr. Køter made few contacts with Jews, but he was visited on the seventh by Dr. Secher, chief anæsthetist at the Copenhagen University Hospital. 'Do you know,' Secher asked, 'that Jews are living in the cellars of their own homes all over Copenhagen?'

'They won't be able to hide for long,' Køster replied gloomily. 'Food rationing will force them out.'

But for the first time Køster realized that many Jews had not been caught by the Germans. Although the Gestapo had looked everywhere, because of Duckwitz's warning, less than a few hundred of the eight thousand Danish Jews the Gestapo had catalogued had been arrested.

Køster and Secher recalled that although Denmark has a State-subsidized Church, few Danes are churchgoers. Any Danes in trouble, the doctors decided, would probably call on their family doctors. Why not contact as many general practitioners as possible, ask them to locate the Jews they knew, and tell the doctors to have these people keep in touch with Bispebjerg? Køster and doctors on the staffs of many other Copenhagen hospitals began calling on family doctors, and nearly all the physicians seemed to be in touch with Jews in hiding. Now the problem was how to save these people. Dr. Secher said his hospital could arrange the boats if the Bispebjerg doctors could have the passengers ready.

Bispebjerg Hospital's buildings sprawl over many wooded acres; and large buildings enclose the hospital's grounds somewhat like a walled city. Its main buildings, like those of almost any major hospital, are connected by long tunnels. Since no

German troops used the hospital, it was an ideal collecting point for the Jews.

On 8th October Dr. Køster arranged to have a canvas-covered lorry come to the hospital to take the first group of Jews to fishing boats Secher's colleagues would have waiting.

The two doctors again contacted the local practitioners, telling them that the Jews were to come to the hospital in the morning, to wear dark clothes, and to ask to be shown to the chapel deep inside the hospital grounds. They must pretend to be coming to a funeral. Altogether about forty Jews were expected.

All morning the hospital head porter directed refugees to the chapel where a young intern waited to welcome them. Many of them worried and confused, some of the Jews arrived on foot from the nearby tram stop, and many came in taxis. By the time Dr. Køster was able to visit the chapel he found the pews crowded by at least eighty people—old and young, grand-parents and infants. Koster and the interne selected about twenty-five and led them outside to the lorry, saw them aboard, and lowered the canvas curtain to shut them in. As the lorry rolled away Køster saw a small hand poke out around the canvas to wave farewell.

To keep the rest of these Jews in the chapel too long on that bright and sunny day would be risky, so Køster began leading small groups down a wooded lane to the hospital's psychiatric building. In a lecture room in the basement they were to wait until the doctors could decide what to do with them. About fifty more Jews arrived at Bispebjerg that afternoon. How to house them inconspicuously? This was the doctors' first ex-perience of underground work, and they were groping their way. By ten o'clock that night the hospital had managed to send about eighty people to boats arranged by a doctor Køster knew on the island of Arnager, but that still left about a hundred people, and Køster knew he could not send them away.

Outside the main grounds of the hospital were the nursing sisters' blocks of flats; senior nurses each had a two-room flat, and juniors were paired in such apartments. There the nursing sisters somehow managed to find accommodation for all of the fugitives.

Køster became worried when he noticed that some of his refugees were obviously not Jews. Some of them later confessed they were Resistance people on the run. But could they also be fugitives from less pardonable crimes? Or Gestapo plants? Perhaps the Germans would raid the hospital at any time. But even if Køster had had experience with security techniques, there was no time to sort out the people who had dumped themselves on him.

In the morning most of the refugees were taken to boats, but by now a slow, though regular stream of Jews was flowing into Bispebjerg. Køster and other doctors in Copenhagen decided that at least several thousand more must still be at large in the city. Their estimate was accurate. The Lyngby group was regularly transporting people out of the country, as were the students' group, Staffeldt's bookshop, and almost every other Dane who could help in this dangerous movement. The Germans, almost totally unaware of what was happening, assumed that eventually Danish Jews would have to come out of hiding for food and would be caught.

At Bispebjerg the doctors felt they must publicize their work in the right quarters in order to attract Jews who needed help, but the Germans must not know what was happening. There had to be a clean break somewhere along the hospital's escape route, and the logical place for that break proved to be in the nursing sisters' quarters.

All Jews arriving at the hospital were shown to the flat of the head matron where someone would try to make certain that the escapees were genuine. Then the people would be hidden in other sisters' flats until transport could be set up. Fairly new buildings, the sisters' blocks of flats had snug, warm cellars—good temporary billets when other flats were too crowded. Later, when the sisters' quarters were full, the hospital hid some Jews in nearby private houses. Many of the nursing sisters stopped reporting to their wards and worked full time with the refugees. Records of the people had to be kept, and passengers had to be selected according to the form of transport, for it would not do to send old people or very small children on boats that made the crossing roughly. On scraps of paper the nursing sisters kept track of everything.

Somehow the hospital would also have to provide bedding and clothing for these people—and food. Dr. Køster was called in by one of the hospital supervisors who asked: 'These meals you're ordering, doctor—who'll pay for them?'

'Oh, just charge them to me,' Køster answered airily.

'Can you pay for *all* of them?'

'Well, no, I can't,' Køster confessed. 'But I suppose you have to charge them to somebody.'

The supervisor smiled sympathetically. 'Yes, I suppose we do.' No bill was ever rendered, and nobody in the hospital's kitchens spoke about the large quantities of food being consumed that October.

Other hospitals in Copenhagen kept finding boats to carry out the Jews, but many fishermen still wanted more money than seemed reasonable. The Contagious Disease Hospital's staff was able to find fishermen who would not charge too much, but the doctors needed more money than they could raise among themselves. Dr. Steffen Lund of Copenhagen's Central Patients' Admission Office began approaching large business firms and factories. Merely claiming he needed money for 'our suffering countrymen', Lund raised many thousands of kroner, and the Danish Medical. Association also donated money. Sometimes Dr. Lund received as much as fifty or sixty thousand kroner from a single source—yet he never

dared tell how or why the money was being spent. Soon
the doctors at Bispebjerg Hospital had collected more than a
million kroner which they hid in the oven in the chief matron's
flat.

Danish Red Cross ambulances transported many of the
fugitive Jews from the hospital; if stopped along the way by
German patrols, the ambulance drivers were to explain that
their passengers were lunatics being transferred from one
asylum to another. Many Jews were also moved away from
Bispebjerg Hospital in taxis, because almost unlimited numbers
of cabs could be driven into the hospital's grounds without
arousing notice. The Copenhagen taxi companies were
secretly alerted never to send to the hospital cabs driven by
drivers who might be pro-German. The fares were always paid
from the chief matron's oven.

Jewish refugees flowed smoothly through Bispebjerg Hospital's escape routes before the month was half over. So many
different groups of Danes seemed to be helping Jews that
quite often individual refugees did not even know who the
people were who got them to safety. Clandestine boat fares
were finally set at about 500 kroner per passenger, but when
Jews came to Bispebjerg without money the physicians
helped them from the oven.

Not all of the escape attempts were rewarded with success,
however. One of the other groups transporting refugees took
about two hundred to a wood along the coast near the North
Sealand resort town of Gilleleje. After dark these people walked
down to the beach and used an electric torch to signal to a
large boat they thought was their transport. The boat drew in
toward the beach and began to play a searchlight back and forth
on the shore. Then the vessel swung about, revved up its
engines, and headed back out to sea. It was a German patrol
vessel—as the Jews realized too late.

The men in charge of this party moved quickly to get the

refugees away before the Gestapo could sweep down. They were taken to a nearby church, and led up the stairs to the only safe hiding place, the tall attic, where for hours they huddled together in the dark. Their refuge, however, turned into a trap when a Danish woman, no doubt well paid for her trouble, informed upon them to the German searchers. Troops surrounded the church, and before anyone could escape, the entire group was arrested and eventually shipped to Theresienstadt.

Another group of Jews were taken to Amager to board a boat within view of a large hotel. In the hotel bar, overlooking the quay, several German Army officers were drinking. A young lieutenant glanced out of the window, saw the scurrying people, watched them for a moment, and then rushed excitedly to his superior officer. 'Sir, there are people out there climbing into boats!'

'So?' the officer asked, taking another sip from his drink.

'But, sir, I think they're Jews! Escaping—'

'Can't you see I'm having a drink?' the senior officer snapped.

'But Jews—escaping—getting away—'

'Dammit! Those people are the Gestapo's responsibility, not ours!' the officer raged. 'Now let me finish my drink in peace.' That group fled without being stopped.

One party of Jews sent from Bispebjerg also had difficulties. Fifty taxis were ordered to the hospital and lined up outside the nursing sisters' quarters while 150 refugees were placed in them. The taxis moved through Copenhagen down to a hook of land near Rødvig, due south of the capital. On a lonely coast road the taxis stopped and the Jews and their doctor escorts alighted to await the boat. As a precaution, the taxis were told to stand by. From over the water the people heard the hollow chugging of a small ship, and when its silhouette appeared through the mist one of the doctors signalled to it. The boat's answer was a burst of gunfire. It was a German coastguard vessel.

'Back into the taxis!' one of the doctors ordered, climbing into the first one himself. As soon as the cars were loaded they raced inland toward a large manor house the Resistance often used as a hiding place for people awaiting shipment out of the country. A doctor telephoned Bispebjerg and asked that food for the 150 people be sent down to the manor house. The food arrived and no questions were asked.

In his taxi the leader of the doctors raced to the south tip of Sealand, then crossed over to the island of Møn. He was in a hurry—a terrible hurry. In a small port he found a trawler. 'Quick!' he shouted to a fisherman on board. 'Sell me your boat!'

The fisherman stared back blankly.

'Hurry up, man! I've no time to waste! What's your boat worth?'

Without hesitating, the fisherman drawled, 'A hundred and fifty thousand kroner. But—'

The doctor was already reaching in his pockets and pulling out large wads of notes. Rapidly he counted out the money—150,000 kroner. Sending away the taxi, he climbed aboard what was now his group's trawler and told the fisherman to set out for Sealand.

Many hours later all fifty of the taxis reported back to the chief matron's flat at Bispebjerg. 'Our meters are still running,' one of the cab drivers grinned, 'and that jaunt cost you three hundred kroner for each of our cabs.'

As Dr. Køster went to the oven for the money the taxi drivers' spokesman explained that the 150 Jews had been put aboard the trawler and were by then probably in Sweden.

Toward the end of October transport was even more per-fectly organised, and Danish customs boats, harbour patrol

launches, police boats, and lighthouse inspection craft were all
carrying out Jews without charge. Contact was made through
a Danish shipping agent to get refugees on to freighters, and
the risk of sending Jews on the smaller trawlers was no longer
necessary.

Several big Finnish ships managed to smuggle twenty Jews
on each run they made from Denmark to Sweden. Only a few
Jews, who had refused to believe the seriousness of the Gestapo
threat, were taken by the Germans, as were about twenty of the
young refugees who, handicapped by their inability to speak
Danish well, tried to escape by passing as Danes. By the end of
October there were almost no Jews left in Denmark, and many
groups such as the Bispebjerg one now began to use their
knowledge of illicit transport to get other Danish refugees out
of the country. Many of the nurses worked at this until the
end of the war, and Dr. Køster had no more time for surgery
until, toward the end of 1943, he had to flee to England, where
he served in the R.A.M.C.

Altogether Denmark sent 7,200 Jews to Sweden; only 570
were captured and sent to Theresienstadt. The Danish welfare
ministries asked the Germans for permission to send food and
clothing parcels to the concentration camp, but after permission
was denied the officials learned that private individuals who
had sent parcels to the Jews had received signed receipts. So the
ministry took money from a secret government source, bought
parcels, and sent them regularly to the camp in the guise of
private gifts. Only about fifty Danish Jews died in the concentration camp, and some of these were old people who might
have died even had they not been incarcerated. The Bispebjerg
Hospital could account for all of the nearly million kroner
spent getting about 2,000 Jews out of the country without
losing a single person—more than were transported by any
other cell. Mogens Staffeldt's bookshop also moved out a
great number, as did the Lyngby group, the students, and
others. Since the groups co-operated freely with each other,

no single unit deserves more credit than another. What was important was that Denmark, Hitler's canary, was the only German-occupied country in which almost the entire population worked to save its Jewish countryman—and succeeded.

A typical selection of newspapers, books and pamphlets published by the Resistance in Denmark

A still from a Resistance film showing Danish women binding illegal newspapers

Illegal newspapers being printed in the basement of a German-occupied hotel in Copenhagen

Pastor Sandbæk after his arrival in England

From a van disguised as a Gestapo vehicle a Resistance newsreel cameraman took this photograph of two colleagues disarming a German soldier in daylight in occupied Copenhagen

On such German-erected barricades in Copenhagen the Danes hung signs: THIS NAZI WEARS NO TROUSERS

An S.S. man orders a Danish policeman to take the name and address of a young Copenhagen girl for wearing an R.A.F. roundel on her cap

A Jutland railway saboteur filmed at work by a Resistance film unit

Such sights as this overturned locomotive were proof of the effectiveness of the railway saboteurs

German soldiers guard Jutland railway repair gangs when saboteurs are heard in the woods

Danes and Germans inspect a sabotaged railway tower

The first Mosquito hits Shell House (in the lower right of this photograph) and veers away before its bombs detonate

Shell House burning after the raid

May 1945. Copenhagen greets Montgomery

8
Exporting a Genius

WHEN they see him do such things as use an entire box of matches to light a single pipeful of tobacco, his compatriots say that Professor Niels Bohr lives in some vague atomic world of his own. Because so few Danes comprehend his work, they like to think of Dr. Bohr as a kindly prototype of the absent-minded professor, and sometimes they forget that, in addition to being in the van in developments in his field of research, this greatest of Danes quotes poetry, reads detective novels as well as the classics, was once an outstanding athlete, and has always taken an active interest in world politics.

In 1942 Dr. Bohr was secretly invited west to help with a new project in America. Having taught or worked with nearly every leading nuclear physicist in the world, he must have known what that project was, but he felt at the time that he would be more useful in Copenhagen, evaluating reports sent him by the Danish military attaché in Berlin, and generally keeping an eye on Nazi scientific developments. The Germans hardly bothered with him at all; they did not understand the professor. For the same reason they kept away from his 10-million-volt cyclotron, an apparatus that incorporated, among other things, an electro-magnet with a 35-ton iron core. But had the Nazis staged a surprise raid on Jacobsen House, the home provided for Dr. Bohr by the Carlsberg Brewery's scientific foundation, they would have found his desk cluttered with damning memoranda. In his quiet way, Dr. Bohr was helping to organize the movement of many refugees out of Denmark.

79

Neither Professor Bohr nor the Resistance knew it, but in August, 1943, a special Gestapo agent was sent to Copenhagen to arrest the physicist. Incredible as it may seem, this German was reluctant to act before calling in a Nazi specialist in nuclear physics, and Bohr was still free in October. Then, more worried that he might somehow be forced into serving the Germans, the Allied authorities sent Bohr a second, more imperative invitation. The professor at once burned all his papers on refugee movements, and through Dr. Lindstrøm-Lang, a scientist in his staff, made plans to take Mrs. Bohr, their three sons, and their families to Sweden. None of the Resistance people who were to help get him away knew why Bohr was being evacuated, but they guessed it was because he had some Jewish ancestors.

In south Copenhagen, near the Sound, there is an area known as 'Music City' because all its streets are named after famous composers. There, one night early in October, Dr. Lindstrøm-Lang took the physicist and his wife, and the professor's famous brother, mathematician Harald Bohr, and his wife. They waited with some other refugees in a house on Mozartvej, and later were led through back streets to a small quay where a fishing boat, the *Søstjernen*, lay tied.

An air raid alert had just sounded and searchlights raked the moonless sky. Niels Bohr was shown into the cramped cabin with some other passengers, but several of the refugees had to be hidden among the herring boxes on the boat's deck. While Christian Hansen, the fisherman owner of the craft, fidgeted with the small, one-cylinder diesel engine, there was some rifle fire on shore. The refugees whispered tensely together, wondering if their flight had been discovered. On deck, Hansen nervously cursed over his engine when it refused to start.

The shooting continued for some minutes and then died away, and the passengers sighed in relief as they heard the engine throb into life, making the entire boat shudder as she nosed out on to the choppy water.

The least perturbed person on board was Niels Bohr; despite the lurching, he dozed for six hours until Hansen cut the engine and the fishing boat drifted. They had only come as far as the middle of the Sound, and again the passengers tensed when they heard low voices call out from a larger boat closing rapidly with them. Why, they wondered, if a patrol ship had intercepted them, did *Søstjernen* not veer off and try to make a quick run for Sweden?

Men from the larger vessel stepped across to the deck of *Søstjernen* and ordered the passengers to gather their things and come on to the other boat—she was crewed by Danish Resistance men. When the last of the refugees had been transshipped, Hansen returned to Copenhagen, rather proud that his craft with the name that meant 'The Starlight' had carried a most Stellar passenger.

The Danes across the Sound had made elaborate preparations for Professor Bohr's arrival, but the customs official who met the boat had not been told to expect the physicist. Sleepily tugging on his clothes as the refugees entered his office, the Swede asked for the people's names, and when he heard 'Niels Bohr', he embarrassedly jerked the straps of his braces over his shoulders. The others would have to await routine questioning, he said, but Professor Bohr was free to catch the next train to Stockholm.

Sweden was then full of German espionage agents, and to avoid attracting their attention the Danes did not arrange private transport to Stockholm for the professor. But when Dr. Bohr climbed aboard his railway carriage a little later, he was followed by a man who kept at a distance and afterwards made no effort on the train to introduce himself to the physicist. All night this man remained alertly on watch outside Dr. Bohr's compartment. When the professor alighted at central station in Stockholm, this man again followed closely behind him. As Bohr lumbered past the ticket gate a round-faced, genial-looking gentleman in civilian clothes

stepped forward and winked at the man who had been following the professor. The round-faced man then went up to the
physicist and introduced himself smartly: 'Lieutenant-Colonel
Gyth, Danish Military intelligence, sir. We have a car for you
outside.'

While they were driving through the city the officer explained that final arrangements had been made to fly Bohr to
England that night. 'Oh, but I have some imperative business
here before I go,' Dr. Bohr said.

Gyth then told him that special guards would be with him at
all times, and that the Germans must not know that the professor
was in Sweden. Bohr agreed that this was a good idea.

The following day the entire Bohr family reached Stockholm except one of the professor's sons who, after an anxious
delay owing to transport difficulties, arrived several days later.
As part of Colonel Gyth's elaborate security arrangements,
Professor Bohr did not live with his family in Stockholm but
was allowed to visit them each day; he was moved between the
homes of several eminent Danes in Stockholm each night.

Professor Bohr decided that, before leaving for England, he
would make use of his notoriety to coax high-ranking Swedes
to get their Government to protest formally to the Germans
about the treatment of Danish jews. Bohr wanted the Germans
told that Danish Jews would be given shelter in the neutral
country. To this end, he had several talks with the Swedish
Foreign Minister. This official, however, was reluctant to take
any action, and because of this Bohr did not feel himself free to
leave for England.

During their discussions with the professor Ebbe Munck and
other prominent free Danes were disturbed to learn that the
professor had forgotten quite a few papers in Jacobsen House.
What did the papers concern? Were they secret scientific
matters, details of refugee movements, or evaluations of intelligence data? Frankly, Bohr confessed, he could not really
remember.

So far, the Germans had not searched Jacobsen House in Copenhagen, but they were likely to do so at any time, so some action had to be taken quickly. Ebbe Munck used his secret communication lines with Denmark to get word to Dr. Lindstrøm-Lang who, quite blithely, went to the Bohr home inside the grounds of the Carlsberg Brewery and asked the housekeeper to show him into Dr. Bohr's solarium study. There Lingstrøm-Lang scooped up all the notes he could find that had been scribbled by the professor, and these were dispatched in a suitcase to Stockholm. Dr. Bohr, still making his appeal to the Swedish Government, found time to go through the mass of notes. To tell the truth, he admitted, he could read none of them and they might have meant anything!

After several days, realizing that the Swedish Foreign Minister was not likely to help him have a protest made to the Germans, Dr. Bohr decided to go to higher authority and called on the Swedish Crown Prince.

Meanwhile, having learned that the physicist was in Sweden, the German Embassy there contacted Copenhagen. The Gestapo men who were sent to search Jacobsen House carried away only stacks of innocuous newspaper cuttings which the professor had saved.

In a later conversation with the Danes in Stockholm Dr. Bohr remembered that he had forgotten a bottle of heavy water in his home. To the Danes, of course, this meant nothing in 1943, and Bohr made no attempt to explain to them what it was; he only said that it was rare and might be important. In any case, he supposed the Germans had found it by then.

Again the Danes contacted Copenhagen and told the Resistance to get the bottle of heavy water from the Bohr home. The house was no longer under German surveillance because the Nazis had ransacked it so thoroughly, and a Resistance agent had no trouble calling on the Bohr housekeeper. Did she know where the professor had left a bottle of something called heavy water? Had the Germans found it?

The woman led the man into the house, but instead of taking him into Dr. Bohr's laboratory, she directed him into her kitchen. Then she went to the larder and reached in among some beer bottles. One bottle held about a quarter of a litre of heavy water. This was sent to Sweden—the last heavy water in Denmark. Probably it would, in any case, have been of little use to the Germans, for they already had taken about twenty tons of the liquid from the Rukan power station in Norway before it was blown up by British saboteurs.

Sweden's Crown Prince received Dr. Bohr graciously and got his Government to send the protest to the Germans about the Danish Jews. Could he, Dr. Bohr's compatriots then asked him, now leave for England? No, he said, not yet. The Swedish protest would mean nothing, Bohr realized, unless it was made public, and he again visited the Crown Prince to explain this to him and ask his help. The protest, the first official action Sweden took against the Germans during the war, was finally published in Swedish newspapers, and Bohr said he was now ready to depart for England.

The escape would by no means be easy. Stockholm aerodrome was used by the Luftwaffe as well as by British aircraft, and the flight to England would be risky. A pair of Mosquito bombers landed in Stockholm every day and departed every night for Britain, a single passenger in a specially constructed seat in the bomb bay of each aircraft. This was how Bohr was to be taken to England, and on the night set for his evacuation the physicist was escorted to the aerodrome by a secretary from the Danish Legation.

Bohr, dressed in warm clothes, was helped into the tight bomb bay, strapped into the seat, and given a flying helmet, headphones, and an oxygen mask. The secretary wished him good-bye, and the aeroplane taxied down the runway. The secretary watched the take-off, then decided he would wait at the aerodrome for a while before returning to his home in the city. Half an hour later the Mosquito landed again at the field;

engine trouble had forced it back. Dr. Bohr would have to wait until the next night to get to England.

The Germans dared take no direct action against Bohr while he was in Sweden, but they were looking everywhere for him, hoping to prevent his leaving. A naturalized Swede, German by birth, reported to Nazi espionage agents in Stockholm that he had seen Bohr at the aerodrome. At the time the Danes did not know of this security leak. Whether it was a result of the information the Germans received is not known—but one of the two Mosquito bombers that left Stockholm the following night never reached England.

On this next evening Bohr was again strapped into a Mosquito's bomb bay and the aircraft took off. This time it did not return.

As the Mosquito climbed toward a safe flying altitude the pilot switched on the intercom and told the professor and the navigator to turn on their oxygen gear. The aircraft continued to climb to between 27,000 and 30,000 feet. A little while later, looking at his instruments, the pilot became alarmed. Something was very wrong. Dr. Bohr's oxygen equipment was not working. The pilot was now very concerned, but his orders were not to turn back, and while they were in the air there was no way to get to the passenger's seat in the bomb bay.

The only thing to do was to keep on toward Britain. However, after passing over Jutland the pilot dived, and from then they flew on at a much lower altitude.

When the plane at last touched down, its worried pilot rushed under the fuselage to open the bomb bay. The physicist was slumped over in his seat, his eyes shut. Aware of the effects of high-altitude flying without proper oxygen, the pilot was very much afraid that his precious passenger might be dead, or, if still alive, that his brain cells would be seriously damaged.

However, when the airman tapped him, Bohr awakened. He had, he said, slept through the entire flight. He had been unable to fit his headphones down over his flying helmet and had not heard the instruction to use his oxygen mask. With it still in his lap, he had dozed.

After some months in Britain, Professor Bohr was taken to America where, for about a year and a half, he worked on the atomic bomb project. During this time he was kept under security guard and was not allowed to use his own name. His colleagues on the Los Alamos project did their best to keep other people from knowing who the famous Dane was, but many stories have been told about the problems American security officers had in guarding the physicist. According to one story, Bohr was taken to New York City to consult with some scientists, and when walking down the street one day he encountered a lady from Copenhagen. 'Why, hello, Dr. Bohr!' she said. 'I didn't know you were in America.'

'I'm very sorry,' Bohr said, for once mindful of security regulations, 'but you're mistaken. My name isn't Bohr.'

'Oh, but you're Niels Bohr. I knew you in Copenhagen.'

'I'm very sorry, madam,' the professor replied, 'I'm *not* Niels Bohr.' Then his eyes brightened. 'But how are you, Mrs. Hansen?'

9

Liquidation

THE pistols' barrels were about an inch and a quarter in diameter and just under a foot long; their triggers were bent metal tubing, and their entire handgrips unclipped and were magazines for 7.65-mm. bullets. A knurled wheel attached to their bolts had to be half-twisted, pulled back, then forced home before each shot—often jamming cartridges behind the chambers and making the pistols misfire. These pistols' only virtue was that they made no more noise than a slap on the wrist. Although mass-produced in Britain during World War II, none of these silent weapons has been displayed in armament museums, for they were created specifically for the unmentionable assassination of traitors. Altogether about 150 reached Denmark during the occupation.

'Well, where do you suppose we can sleep tonight?' Jens Lillelund asked. He and the man called John, returning from a sabotage job on the evening of 8th December, 1943, had been warned to keep away from their homes that night.

'I know a Norwegian lady, a dressmaker,' John said. 'Some of the men have been hiding in her flat on and off for six months.'

'Can she be trusted?' Lillelund asked.

'Absolutely.'

The two men cycled out to a grubby back street a few blocks behind the Trianglen traffic intersection; no trees, only dark, old-fashioned blocks of flats lined each side of Faksegade. Locking their bicycles, the pair entered the drab brown hallway of number 4, and rang a bell on the ground floor. A moment later a blonde woman drew back the glass-panelled door a few inches.

'Mrs. Delbo,' John asked, 'can you put us up for the night?'

'Of course. I always have beds for loyal Danes.'

Smiling, she led them into the flat, down a narrow hallway, and into a room cluttered with pieces of cloth, packets of pins, spools of thread, a sewing machine, and women's clothes basted together. 'Excuse the mess,' the tall, handsome woman apologized to John, 'but do sit down and introduce me to your friend.'

'Hedwig Delbo, Mr. Finsen,' John said, using Lillelund's cover name of the moment.

Lillelund guessed Mrs. Delbo was about thirty-five. 'Finsen? The leader of Holger Danske ?' she asked in astonishment.

Frowning, Lillelund nodded, then shot a questioning glance at John.

John smiled; he trusted Mrs. Delbo.

The Norwegian woman fed the two men, gave them a place to sleep, then promised to awaken them in the morning.

The saboteurs were dressed and ready to leave before eight o'clock. 'Oh, but don't rush away,' Mrs. Delbo protested. 'Let me go out and get some milk, and we can have breakfast.'

'Thanks, but we'd better move along,' answered Lillelund.

'I'll only be gone a minute. I can get milk just across the street.' Mrs. Delbo, already tugging on her coat, was going toward the door.

A few minutes later, when she did not come back, Lillelund said, 'Come on, let's go. No use wasting time here. This sort of thing can be dangerous.'

Outside the men unlocked their bicycles, and cycled to the right, toward the corner. Turning left into Odensegade, they noticed a large black saloon pointed toward Trianglen and parked in front of a newspaper shop. Lillelund and John looked at each other. It was a petrol-driven motor-car, and petrol was reserved for the Germans and the police alone.

As they cycled over the smooth cobblestones in Odensegade they heard from behind them the whine of a starter motor, then the car easing after them. Lillelund glanced over his shoulder, look at John, and asked: 'Gestapo?'

'Yes!'

'Don't look back,' Lillelund ordered, 'and don't try to race away from them. When we get to the corner, veer right, go around the traffic island, then sharp left down Østerbrogade.'

People cycling to work filled the wide boulevard, but the traffic lights favoured the two men, and they skimmed around the traffic island without having to stop. The large black saloon turned left at the same time as the saboteurs but began heading down past Trianglen and away from them. Then it came to a stop, backed up, turned around, and was again just behind the two men as they cycled down Østerbrogade.

'What do you think?' John asked.

'They're following us,' Lillelund said.

John was pedalling faster now. 'Let's cut down here,' he said, turning right at the next corner.

Lillelund was just behind. 'This is a bad street, John! There aren't any turnings off it for quite a distance.'

The black saloon was following them closely.

'Draw up just ahead,' Lillelund ordered, 'and we'll try to double back past them.'

Both men wheeled their cycles around excitedly and raced back the way they had come, past the car. It stopped, roared and turned around. 'Quickly!' Lillelund called.

The two pedalled side-by-side toward Østerbrogade. Perhaps they could lose themselves in the heavy bicycle traffic.

Suddenly Lillelund heard shots and shouting from the car, then, glancing to his right, saw John reach under his jacket.

'Don't waste time!' Lillelund shouted. 'You can't shoot a pistol from a bicycle! Hurry! Let's try to get away !'

But John—not trying to draw a pistol—held his hand under his jacket.

At the corner of Østerbrogade John swerved toward the right, but Lillelund steered straight through the traffic, across the wide boulevard, and up Rosenvængets Allé, the street on the other side. After passing the police station, he noticed another black car parked just before the corner of Faksegade. Shooting past, Lillelund heard it start and swerve around. He knew it was following him.

No time to stop. Lillelund pumped the pedals as hard as he could and the bicycle jittered over the cobbles—past blocks of flats, then large houses that had once been suburban villas when Copenhagen was smaller. The saloon followed, the men in it leaning out the windows and yelling. Jens Lillelund remembered that at the end of Rosenvængets Allé there was a short path, wide enough for a cycle but not a car. He turned abruptly down this path and, hidden by the tall buildings from the sight of his pursuers, finally succeeded in giving them the slip.

Within an hour Lillelund had gathered together some Holger Danske men who told him that after he pedalled away toward his escape across Østerbrogade, John rounded the corner and toppled from his bicycle, a bullet through his chest, another through his leg. As the Gestapo car came up behind him, John began firing his pistol toward its windscreen, killing one of the Germans, wounding the other. A number of their bullets hit him and he fainted.

The second Gestapo car, having lost Lillelund at the top of Rosenvængets Allé, sped back to Østerbrogade. One of the Germans got out, picked up John's pistol from the cycle path, and hammered the badly wounded saboteur on the head, then picked him up and threw him over the bonnet of the black saloon as a hunter might a deer. John, bleeding badly, possibly already dead, was taken to prison.

'There had to be an informer in this,' Lillelund said firmly.

'Any idea who?' one of the saboteurs asked.

'Nobody knew where John and I were going except us. What about this Mrs. Delbo?' Lillelund asked.

'But a Norwegian—' one of the others said. 'After all—'

'We have to find out,' Lillelund said, 'before we can decide what to do next. We must be absolutely sure.

Quickly the men formulated a plan that would either clear or. condemn the Norwegian dressmaker. It began with a telephone call that same morning.

'Hello. Mrs. Delbo? This is Mr. Finsen. I suppose you know John was taken this morning.'

'Oh, no! That's terrible! Are you all right? What are you going to do now?' Mrs. Delbo's voice was tight and tearful.

'I'm all right, but I've got to get to Sweden tonight. Staying in Denmark would be suicidal for me. I'd like to see you before I go.

'Where are you now?' Did he hear an expectant note in her voice? Lillelund did not want to have an opinion.

'I'll be at your flat at three o'clock this afternoon.'

A pair of young lovers strolled into Faksegade shortly before three o'clock that afternoon, moving slowly, stopping for long minutes in the few doorways along the street. They seemed barely to notice two black, petrol-driven saloons, one at either end of the block—and in front of number 4, a hand cart covered with Christmas trees. A man in a black leather trench-coat strode from one of the cars to the handcart, to speak with the tree-seller. The young lovers strolled close enough to the cart to see, under the Christmas trees, a sub-machine gun.

The girl, an eighteen-year-old university student, knew Mrs. Delbo by sight, Like the young man with her, she worked for Holger Danske.

When some Resistance men met later that evening to listen to the young man and woman, they decided Mrs. Delbo must be liquidated. Denmark has long been out of the habit of executing people for crimes and, had it been possible, the Resistance would have imprisoned informers, but organized resistance would have collapsed if such people were not destroyed—to silence them, and to warn other weak Danes not to sell information to the Germans. Who would kill Mrs. Delbo?

One of the men blew his nose—he had a bad cold—and spoke up: 'There've been nights when I've stayed at her flat, too, and what happened to John could have happened to any of us. I'll do it.'

'Don't be crazy!' one of the others said. 'What if you miss and she recognizes you? Let somebody else do it!'

'No,' the man said, 'it's my job. Get me a silent pistol.'

Two afternoons later a newsvendor looked out of his shop window on the Odensegade corner of Faksegade. On grey winter afternoons Faksegade is usually deserted, but now about twenty young men loitered in the doorways as far as Rosenvængets Allé, and just before four o'clock a man arrived, blowing his nose. Whatever was happening, the newsvendor did not like it—so he telephoned for help.

The man with the silent pistol saw Danish police rush into Faksegade from Rosenvængets Allé. Turning to run the other way, he saw more police enter the street from Odensegade. He ran into a block of flats opposite Mrs. Delbo's. An old woman answered his tap at a ground-floor doorway, and he shoved past her, slamming the door shut behind him. On a table was a telephone, and with a knife he cut its line, then apologized to the old woman and her husband, tossed them money to have their telephone repaired, and went to the front window. Police in the street were arresting some of his guards, and across from his window, shuffling about in her living-room, he could see Hedwig Delbo, unaware of the commotion.

When the police had gone the saboteur sneaked away, crossed Copenhagen, and met some of his comrades. 'We have to try again in a hurry,' he said, 'before she has a chance to find out we're after her. No guards this time.'

.   .   .   .   .

While the man with a cold drove back toward Faksegade with two other saboteurs in a stolen Gestapo car, other members of the group telephoned the Rosenvængets Allé police station, explained that the six or seven youths who had been arrested were mostly naval cadets, not criminals but Resistance men. They were permitted to escape through the police station's back door.

'Your cold must be killing you. Your eyes are watering terribly,' one of the men driving the car told the man with the silent pistol. 'Are you sure you're well enough to do the job?'

'Perfectly sure,' He was bothered not, by his cold but by the picture of Hedwig Delbo placidly sewing dresses, unaware someone was on the way to shoot her. Sabotage is one thing, but liquidation. . . .

Parking the car some distance away, the three men walked toward Mrs. Delbo's flat. All blackout curtains had been drawn for the night, and Faksegade was deserted. The man with the cold blew his nose a final time, pocketed his handkerchief, and pulled out the silent pistol. He half turned the knurled wheel, drew back the bolt, felt a bullet slide home. Then he left his friends and rapped at Mrs. Delbo's door.

The Norwegian woman's face broke into an embarrassed smile. 'W-w-w-why, hello! Do come in.

Turning, she preceded him down the corridor, but the man, standing still, raised the pistol. Fifteen feet away Hedwig Delbo opened the living-room door and turned. Her mouth opened in a gasp, and she pushed the back of a clenched fist to her teeth. Her scream covered the pistol's slap, and she crumpled forward. The man tried to ready the pistol for another shot, but the bullet jammed, and Mrs. Delbo looked very dead, anyway, so he turned and ran, his temples throbbing. His cold was turning into flu.

The Resistance later telephoned the Rosenvængets Allé police station to look for Mrs. Delbo, and at nine that evening the man with a cold went to see a friend in the central police station.

'*Idiot!*' the policeman yelled at the saboteur. 'That woman you think you killed is in the next room screaming your name and demanding to see the Gestapo. Get out of here—quickly!'

The next morning his police friends contacted the saboteur; hundreds of copies of his photograph, they warned him, were being circulated. He went into hiding until he was able to get to Sweden a few weeks later.

Mrs. Delbo also hid, and although all Resistance people in the city looked for her, she seemed to have vanished. Then, early in January, a man in the Copenhagen office of Thomas Cook's, the travel agents, telephoned a Resistance contact. Hedwig Delbo was leaving Cook's office at six o'clock that evening for a Lufthansa aeroplane to Norway.

Killing the woman inside the travel agency would have compromised the Resistance contact there, but Cook's agreed to let the assassin run back into their office, around the old-fashioned counters, and out through a back door that led into Tivoli. The pleasure garden's manager would have one of Tivoli's rear exits unlocked. The young man who was to kill Mrs. Delbo decided to go to the travel agency in a car which he would also be able to use for his getaway.

Driving into the centre of Copenhagen toward Cook's office, he had a flat tyre, and by the time he changed the wheel, it was past six o'clock. Ditty and sweating, he rushed into Cook's.

'She left five minutes ago,' the contact told him. 'We had no way to detain her.'

Three tries on her life, and now Mrs. Delbo was out of Denmark. The Special Operations Executive in London was notified of the failure, and in Bergen Norwegian Resistance men shot at Hedwig Delbo, but her life seemed charmed, for they too failed to kill her.

Near death, John lay in a Copenhagen prison cell, his eight

bullet wounds festering badly. The bullet that had torn through his thigh had shattered the bone completely, and the Nazis not only failed to set the break, but they jarred and bent the man's leg to try to torture him into giving the names of other Holger Danske men. Because he refused to talk, the Germans would not let John leave his cell, and his mattress became a clotted mass of fetid contamination. A Danish doctor named Jørgen Kieler who was a prisoner in the same cell did his best to nurse the Resistance man, washing the wound with the only liquid available, dirty potato soup.

The Norwegian Resistance sent word to Denmark that Hedwig Delbo, now afraid to stay in her native land, was returning to Copenhagen. Every Resistance man in the city began looking for her, but for a few months the woman managed to stay hidden. Then Mogens Staffeldt received a telephone call from another Copenhagen bookseller. 'I think I've seen her. A Norwegian-speaking woman came into my shop for a book from our lending library. Looked like Mrs. Delbo.'

'What name did she use? Where does she live?' Staffeldt asked.

'That's just it. When I told her the book was out, I asked if I could send it to her, but she got nervous and said she'd call again.'

'When she comes back,' Staffeldt said, 'try to get her name and address.'

Several days later the bookseller telephoned Staffeldt a second time. 'The Norwegian woman was here again. I told her we expect the book soon. She said her name is "Mrs. Dam",' and he quoted the woman's telephone number.

Was this Mrs. Dam really Hedwig Delbo? The Resistance tried to check the telephone number, but it was unlisted. Nevertheless, loyal Danes in Copenhagen's telephone service traced the number to an address in Sankelmarksgade, a small street in south Copenhagen. In the building the Resistance men were surprised to learn that a saboteur from another group rented a room on the same staircase, but above the dressmaker.

The saboteur was even more surprised. 'Here I've been looking for that damned woman everywhere, and she lives in the same house as I do!' he said. He agreed to keep a watch on Mrs. Dam.

But was this Mrs. Delbo? The Resistance group had to be quite sure before they could take action, so Staffeldt called his colleague. 'Telephone Mrs. Dam that you have her book now. Let me know when she's coming for it.'

The Resistance sent two men who knew Mrs. Delbo to park in a car in front of the bookshop, sitting there for hours on the day Mrs. Dam was to collect her book. Several times policemen stopped and stared at their car, and the two saboteurs became nervous.

The woman did not show up, and after a while a pair of policemen walked by, saw the car, turned, and walked directly toward it.

'We'd better go,' the driver said, and started the engine.

They had missed their quarry, for she came to the shop shortly after they drove away. The policemen, they learnt afterwards, had been curious about the car because it had no petrol ration stamp on its windscreen, and they wondered if the men in it were criminals, saboteurs, or Gestapo men.

Without revealing their hand, the Resistance had to find out if Mrs. Dam was the woman they wanted, and only one person could learn this without arousing suspicion. The young girl who had posed as a lover in Faksegade offered: 'I'll go to her and order a dress.'

The woman might have German bodyguards, the saboteurs warned the girl, but she said simply, 'I'll be all right.'

On returning to Staffeldt's bookshop she explained, 'This Mrs. Dam is living with another woman who answered the door. When she saw I was alone she let me in and I asked

Mrs. Dam to measure me for a dress. It'll be ready on the ninth of March—and Mrs. Dam is Mrs. Delbo.'

The two men who went with the girl decided not to bother with a silent pistol; both carried automatics that would not jam. In Sankelmarksgade the men entered the building first and climbed to the landing above Mrs. Delbo's flat. At the door of the flat the girl pushed the bell several times, sounding a special combination of rings Hedwig Delbo told her to use. The door opened.

'I'm back for my dress, Mrs. Dam,' the girl said.

At the same moment the two men leaped down the stairs, pushed the young girl aside, and began shooting. The girl was already going down the stairs when the men closed the flat's door behind them, having made quite certain Hedwig Delbo was dead.

The police the Resistance telephoned to fetch Hedwig Delbo found 30,000 kroner in notes in her flat—much more than a dressmaker could amass. News of the liquidation was smuggled into the prison to John. No nearer recovery than he had been earlier, this was little consolation to him. He never told the Germans his comrades' names, and he never walked again. A month later he was dragged out into the prison yard and shot.

10
Strike!

EACH Midsummer Night Danes kindle bonfires, burn effigies of witches, have parties and enjoy firework demonstrations; but German blackouts cancelled the holiday during the occupation. At dusk one evening a week after Midsummer Night, 1944, sudden loud whooshes from Copenhagen's Tivoli amusement park, from the Town Hall Square, and from another square split the city's silence. Rockets flashed skyward, then with a jarring bang showered down a confetti of light over the centre of the city. Crowds in the Town Hall Square watched a firework demonstration as splendid as anything they had seen before the war. When the rockets illuminated Dagmar House, the Nazi headquarters building in a corner of the square, the growing mob applauded, and it roared with laughter when 'Tipperary' and other Allied songs were played over the public address system in the Town Hall's tower. Handbills distributed to the crowd explained that the fireworks were a greeting from fighting Denmark.

The Germans were furious and began retribution in the morning; Dr. Best ordered an eight o'clock curfew. Then, on 26th June, Danish hooligans from the Nazi-led Schalburg Corps visited Tivoli for some of their own special brand of fun. Shortly before two o'clock in the morning Tivoli's concert hall, arena, fun fair, dance pavilion, and Glass Hall were 'Schalburgtaged' (this name, given to such actions which were meant to discredit underground saboteurs, became part of occupied Denmark's vocabulary). Shock waves from the explosions shattered the Hall of Mirrors, trees were uprooted, debris-filled craters replaced buildings, and the Big Dipper was now as unsafe as such conveyances only appear to be. *Information* reported: 'At dawn Tivoli looked as if the Germans had been there.' For good measure, a Schalburg Corps group the same night destroyed many thousands of kroner worth of rare porcelain figures by blowing up a part of the Royal Copenhagen Porcelain Factory.

Copenhagen people were incensed; the curfew had already reduced the time they could spend outdoors enjoying that exceptionally fine summer, and now they had been deprived of their favourite amusement park. Their feeling asserted itself openly in the morning when workers at Burmeister og Wain, Denmark's largest shipyard, held a mass meeting and voted to say in a letter to Dr. Best that, because the curfew denied them evening hours needed to tend vegetable gardens, they would have to finish work each day at noon. To neglect the gardens, the letter claimed, meant starvation.

That evening the centre of Copenhagen was hushed at eight o'clock, but in the suburbs people ignored the curfew to take evening strolls and to visit friends. This was the beginning; the entire city of Copenhagen was going to go on strike against the Germans.

Danish police, following German instructions, rushed around arresting people, taking in about sixty who claimed to have been walking in their sleep. To clear all the streets the police would have had to arrest at least a hundred thousand somnambulists. People ordered to return to their homes told the police: 'You are very nice, but this has nothing to do with you.' In Frederiksberg, to reinforce the Danish police, Wehrmacht patrols rode bicycles through the crowds, firing light machine guns. Townspeople made a sport of lingering on corners as long as they dared before fleeing from the gunfire. To harass the Germans in some streets they built bonfires between tram tracks, burning old newspapers, mattresses, and other rubbish. Barricades of handcarts and bicycles were thrown up to keep the troops out of other streets, and paintings, waste baskets and chamber pots were dumped down on the patrols. The Germans, panicking quickly, began shooting through windows, trying to terrify people into returning to their homes, but, of course, the shooting only worsened matters. On many street corners people talked of a general strike. Six were killed and about fifty were wounded, some seriously, that night.

Resistance sabotage groups in the city took advantage of the chaos to experiment with explosives; they had long wanted to know the smallest quantities of plastic explosive that would split a railway track in two. In Holte, north of Copenhagen, a Nazi ammunition train was derailed. 'Schalburgtage' people were also busy that night, and the watchman in a Conservative Voters' Association headquarters awoke in the morning to find that his bedroom was now an open balcony; the building had been blown up around him.

The dock workers at Burmeister og Wain lived up to their threat and went home the next day at noon. Workers in many smaller businesses commandeered by the Germans also left for home. Department store employees talked of going on strike, and now suddenly every Copenhagener wanted to be sure of eight free hours before curfew time. At night Copenhagen was again quiet in the city centre, and oblivious of the curfew in the suburbs. Bonfires were again kindled, and again where they could the Danish police maintained order, although the Germans did most policing—with patrol cars full of trigger-happy Gestapo men. In some streets German soldiers shot into crowds, and the evening's twelve dead included several women and an eighty-three-year-old retired policeman. An artist and his wife were shot in the doorway of their flat, and in another street a burst of German machine-gun fire tore a man nearly in half. Late at night the Schalburg Corps again struck, this time demolishing a sports pavilion.

·   ·   ·   ·   ·

The next day's legal newspapers stated that the curfew would be tightened that night. Nervous German officials were asking the Danish Foreign Ministry if a three-hour pushing back of the curfew would get three extra working hours from the people. The Foreign Ministry, aware that the Germans already had been deprived of hundreds of thousands of vital Danish man-hours, said they did not know, that the go-slow movement had no official connections. So far the only inconvenience the action had cost most Danes was the absence of rye bread from their tables, for Copenhagen's largest bakery was on strike. But every important business in the city had by now almost reached a halt, either because workers walked out or because Resistance men or Communists telephoned and suggested that shutting down might be a good idea.

At curfew time, to keep German patrols from their streets, townspeople began erecting strong barricades; in front of each barricade was a bonfire, easily a thousand bonfires altogether, flames licking fifteen feet skyward. Wherever the fire brigade extinguished fires, new ones were lit. Swastikas and giant portraits of Hitler burned, and in one place the Führer was hanged, then burned, in effigy. Fuel oil was flooded on to some tram tracks and lit, and snakes of flame trailed down streets. In one street doors were heaped on the fires. Anything inflammable—even the Germans' road markers—burned. The Germans took eight fire engines from the main fire brigade station, but the vehicles' petrol tanks were dry. Blacked-out Copenhagen was clearly visible across the Sound in Malmø. The crowds' shadows dancing witch-like on buildings were a nightmare for the Germans. In all, at least twenty-four people were shot that evening, and two died of their wounds.

Many tramcar motormen and conductors failed to report for work the following day, and when the Germans threatened to take over telephone exchanges, all the operators went home, and the lines went dead. None of the legal newspapers could publish, and because all postal workers had come out on strike by evening, *Information* warned its subscribers that some of them might miss copies of the bulletin, 'for we cannot send bicycle couriers all the way to North Jutland'. More seriously, *Information* cautioned labour union officials that the time had come for them to go underground. Almost every shop and factory in Copenhagen had closed, and at some factories fighting between Danish workers and German guards was serious. A Danish sabotage group had completely demolished a large aluminium factory early in the morning, and the smoke could be seen all over Copenhagen.

Worried that his boss, von Ribbentrop, might visit Denmark on his way home from a tour of inspection in Norway, Dr. Best raged to his staff that he would break Copenhagen, and the doctor paid little attention to the military's suggestion that the Germans might themselves behave less ruthlessly. Even Dr. Best's second-in-command wanted to see the situation handled differently, and all day excited communications were radioed between Copenhagen and Berlin.

The only things that could be purchased easily in the city were bread and milk, for which people formed queues at the back doors of shops since loitering too long in open streets might be suicidal. A few closed food stores were looted, and civilians mobbed a clothing store owned by German sympathizers, smashed its show windows, scattered the merchandise in the streets and burned the building. One of the few tram-cars still running was derailed when a sack of cement was hurled under its wheels, blocking several of the last tram routes still in operation.

Near the central railway station a Danish civilian suddenly took a pistol from his pocket, aimed at a street corner crowd, and squeezed the trigger. The crowd surged toward him, snatched away his pistol, and shouted 'Kill him! Kill him!' He was about to be hanged on a telephone pole when police arrived. Searching the man, the Danes found no identification papers but a lot of ammunition and a large number of food ration coupons. He was, they concluded, one of the terrorists the Gestapo released on Copenhagen from time to time—men who fended for themselves and who would rarely be assisted by the Germans. A carload of steel-helmeted German soldiers finally dispersed the crowd around the man.

Cars full of armed men fanned out from Dagmar House, and at least one of these roamed the city to shoot with abandon into the crowds, sometimes catching motorized patrols of Danish police in the crossfire. At the steps of the central station two men alighted from one of the cars, and as the vehicle roared away the pair shot at anybody in sight.

Setting up two field-guns at a major traffic roundabout, the Germans fired into the crowds, then began throwing hand grenades. But Copenhagen's mobs would not be broken, even when Schalburg men, wearing either Danish police uniforms or other disguises, fired at close range.

At ten o'clock that evening, as the city still throbbed with action, the last suburban trains moved outside Copenhagen and were abandoned by their drivers. All public transport had now stopped. Dr. Best ordered all gas, water, and electricity supplies cut off; and the State Radio closed down. The growing barricades made even bicycling a nuisance as people tore up paving to fence off their streets. A general strike in Odense a year earlier had never been as bad as this—and Copenhagen's worst had not yet begun, although on that day 227 people were wounded, and sixteen died.

By the next day, 1st July, German military police units from all over Sealand moved toward Copenhagen. Only one member of the Freedom Council was in the city, but he got together with the woman editor of *Frit Danmark*, an illegal newspaper, Arne Sejr, and Børge Outze to issue an ultimatum to the Germans stating, among other things, that the strike would stop if the curfew were lifted and the Schalburg Corps were moved out of Copenhagen. The ultimatum gave the strike its first strong purpose. And in case anyone did not know of it, the Resistance began passing out handbills announcing that Copenhagen was striking against the Germans. The underground army ignored German taunts to bring forth weapons for an open battle, for the Resistance was still too poorly equipped. Strangely, Copenhagen's mood was a holiday one, and on a main street someone erected a mock tombstone inscribed, 'Sweet, Sweet Little Adolf.' All the breweries in the city somehow managed to continue production, and beer was plentiful.

Across Rosenørns Allé from the Forum that day Børge Outze saw a small boy thumb his nose at a German sniper. The German raised his rifle, but the youngster had ducked behind a wall before the bullet cracked toward him. Again the boy leaned out, thumbed his nose—and was shot at and missed. After the soldier had almost emptied his rifle, a German officer ordered the shooting to stop, and the little boy, thumbing his nose a final time, ran away.

The bloodiest hours of the strike came on this day when German patrols, blocked by a barricade on Amager Island, flew into a rage and aimed their weapons at houses. At another Amager barricade the Germans extinguished a bonfire, but it was lit again, put out, and re-lit—four times altogether. After midnight the Germans had to call Kastrup Aerodrome for a Luftwaffe fighter to strafe Amager's streets. Amager's hospital admitted sixty-seven bullet-wounded patients in an hour.

All over Copenhagen Germans shot unarmed people— drunks who could not move quickly enough, women and children. Only the very centre of the city was deserted and ghost-like. Where wounded people lay in the streets they were often passed unnoticed; the entire situation was too unreal. Danish Red Cross ambulances cruised back and forth on continual lookout for casualties, for no means existed to report the wounded to a central headquarters. German patrol cars, ignoring the red crosses, fired on the ambulances.

More and more pre-German shops were looted, and a few non-Nazi tobacconists also suffered. A butcher and his assistant who had sold all their meat to the inhabitants of their district were shot by members of the Schalburg Corps and S.S. men, who had come to pick up stores and found the freezers empty. In one street Danes mobbed a German Army warehouse and hung its stores of uniforms on lamp posts or burned them.

Droves of people carried all sorts of containers to the reservoirs for water, and in the State Hospital coffins were being used as storage containers for vegetables because the hospital authorities anticipated a long siege. Red Cross lorries delivered milk to the hospitals for redistribution to parents who produced the baptismal certificates of their small children.

Stark red posters all over Copenhagen the next morning announced that 'martial law had been declared in the city and the immediate suburbs'. Dr. Best said he would bring Copenhagen to its knees and it would never be able to rise again, and although direct control had been taken out of his hands, the Wehrmacht was following his plan to starve out the 700,000 people estimated to be in the city. Until then, all roads leading from Copenhagen had been crowded by people fleeing on foot and in every sort of conveyance—like the roads out of Paris in 1940—but now all traffic in and out of the city had been stopped. Panzer divisions—some sent down from Norway, some brought up from the Reich—ringed the entire city. Danes who approached the blockade, either from within or from outside, were to be shot. Nevertheless, thousands escaped that day—many through sewers. That day *Information* published three issues which were duplicated outside the military zone. Some of the copy was smuggled through the German barricade by the Swedish Ambassador, who had to pay a visit to King Christian, a prisoner in his summer palace at Sorgenfri, north-west of Copenhagen. Much of the copy was telephoned out on a secret line *Information* had somehow managed to keep in operation. The stories quickly reached England and were soon picked up again in Copenhagen by whoever had their battery-operated wireless receivers tuned in on the B.B.C. Danish Service.

Later in the day the Germans began allowing people to enter the city. Then, hoping rail traffic through North Sealand might be resumed, the Germans tried to make Glostrup station, west of Copenhagen, the main rail point, but few trains ran.

From their perimeter blockade the Germans threatened to fire on Copenhagen with 75-mm. guns, hoping to maintain order that way. Copenhagen was in chaos without its gas, water, electricity, telephones, radio, legal newspapers, or public transport. Men of the Schalburg Corps and German troops roamed the streets, in confiscated brewery vans and other lorries, and although the Danish civil police had no authority, they tried feebly to help maintain order.

The Germans began looking for a way to start the flow of electricity again, for the absence of it hurt them as much as the Danes. They also announced that they would try to run the trams again the next day, hoping workers might thus be induced to return to the factories. Dr. Best said that if labour organizations would promise a cancellation of the strike, electricity would flow again at 7 p.m. Shown a list of demands made by Danish union officials, Best was furious, for the message contained a strong criticism of German military conduct in Copenhagen.

Rye bread sold for high black market prices, but most food was still offered at the back doors of shops, and people who could not afford it were allowed unlimited credit. Greengrocers gave away fruit and vegetables, and bakers worked overtime in the smaller bakeries to produce bread which they then distributed free. In courtyards behind blocks of flats large fires for communal meals were built, and people in the flats pooled whatever they had. Thirty-one lorry-loads of meat spoiled that day because no electricity was available to keep refrigeration plants working, and the weather remained hot. A butcher gave away pork, then built a fire behind his shop where his friends roasted their free meat. The war had frightened many Danes into hoarding tinned food, so the fear of immediate starvation was not great. Copenhagen was in no mood to worry about the future.

All schools had now been closed by the strike, and children made a game of going up to the Panzer troops in the Town Hall Square to ask, 'Where can we buy raffle tickets to win these tanks?'

The plundering of Nazi-co-operating shops continued, and the illegal Press reported sympathy strikes in Odense and in many North Jutland towns, none serious enough to be broken by troops. By the day's end the Germans had switched on the electricity again, and the State Radio could broadcast. All night bonfires lit street battles, and German horse-drawn artillery rumbled through the city until dawn.

At half-hourly intervals in the morning the State Radio insisted that the strike was over, but this was not true. The Gestapo armed cars, now nicknamed 'death cars', cruised everywhere, and Schalburg men continued to fire into the crowds. Resistance workers passed out more handbills urging firmness until the Germans met the Freedom Council's demands. Posters all over the city now ordered the people to be peaceful, but in several places Schalburg Corps members shot into groups of townspeople who had stopped to read the notices. A police van with a loudspeaker cruised down a main street ordering the people to be peaceful and to return to work, but one of the 'death cars' trailed the van and shot at people leaning from open windows of houses.

Throughout Copenhagen German soldiers had set up low rings of sandbags at street corners, but when the Wehrmacht soldiers sprawled with rifles in their little fortresses, a wall of hundreds of curious Copenhageners would close in around them. Embarrassed, the infantrymen would quit their positions.

When telephone operators called in at their exchanges to see what was happening, German soldiers ordered the women to their switchboards, and the telephones began working again. By noon, the Germans insisted, the trams would again be running, and the Danish police offered to protect them, but how could anybody find the conductors and motormen? Thousands of people that day were able to sneak past the city's barricades into the countryside, and more reinforcements for the Germans were landed at Kastrup Airport.

Although the Danish Government had resigned nearly a year earlier, the country's non-political ministers had remained at their desks, and one of them, H. H. Koch, the Minister of Labour and Social Welfare, felt the strike must stop before the Germans did something really drastic. Using his brother as courier, Koch got in touch with the Freedom Council, and through him, negotiations were begun with the Germans. This was the first time that Danish officialdom had recognized the existence of the underground Government. In the garden of the Royal Library in Copenhagen several Freedom Council members carefully drafted a statement to the citizens of the city, asking them to return to work.

That night the radio continued saying the strike was already over, but the 'death cars' continued to shoot at innocent people, and after midnight Luftwaffe aircraft droned low over Copenhagen, destroying the city's sleep.

And the next day, 4th July, the city did go peacefully back to work. Some tram routes could not be operated again until their tracks were reset and their overhead wires repaired, and the barricades had to be pulled away. The Freedom Council took credit for the return to work, claiming that their ultimatum had caused the Schalburg Corps to be moved outside the city, the shooting of innocent people to cease, and the curfew to be lifted—but these were things that probably would have happened anyway. The Germans said their last-minute threat to bomb Frederiksberg and Istedgade, one of the most troublesome slum streets where, for several days, banners had taunted the Germans, 'ISTEDGADE NEVER GIVES UP', had finally broken Copenhagen. But since few of the city's people knew of the threat *or* believed it, the Nazi claim was equally weak.

For the first and last time during the occupation Copenhagen had been sufficiently unified to show the canary's spirit. The strike was a phenomenon that grew out of a mood, and nobody except the masses of Copenhagen deserve credit for its beginning and its ending. Some nights as many as five thousand bonfires had burned, many of them lit by old ladies.

As normal life resumed, people tipped their hats as they passed wreaths lain on the street which bore such inscriptions as one in the middle of a busy traffic roundabout: 'To the memory of three Danes who fell here'. *Information* was able to note without exaggeration: 'Score—one for Copenhagen, none for the Germans.'

11
The Canary's Voice

Early in 1942, Thomas Sneum, one of the first two Danes who escaped directly to Britain, was one of the first two Allied agents to return by parachute to Denmark. With them they brought a portable wireless transmitter, and in Copenhagen they met Arne Duus-Hansen, an engineer for the radio firm of Bang og Olufsen, who helped them broadcast their first message to England.

After several months, however, Sneum's presence in Denmark was detected by the Germans, and he fled on foot across the frozen Sound to Sweden in early 1943. Duus-Hansen then helped the next Allied agent who parachuted into Denmark to make radio contact with S.O.E.

Like Sneum, this agent had brought the same sort of broadcasting gear that had been sent to underground organizations in other German-occupied countries. This equipment was entirely unsuited to Denmark's needs because it was too large to be transported without arousing suspicion, and it operated only on alternating current, although at that time nearly all of Copenhagen was supplied with direct current. And worse, the transmitter's valves were mostly of types that could not be replaced in Denmark.

Several more parachutists soon arrived, always with the same sort of cumbersome, impractical transmitters, and what radio contact they could establish with Britain was slow and unreliable. The Danish Resistance, now growing rapidly, needed better radio connections, yet Britain was unable to provide either properly qualified radio operators or the sort of equipment suitable for the job. In an attempt to solve the problems, Duus-Hansen was called to Stockholm to meet representatives from S.O.E. 'Why not,' the Dane suggested, 'let us train our own radio operators?'

A completely unworkable idea, the representatives said, because the job had to be done by men trained in Britain, men who knew the British procedure, men the British were sure would be reliable.

'Nonsense !' Duus-Hansen said. 'Any man who can't tap out and receive, say, a hundred and twenty letters a minute is no good for this job, and you don't have any Danes you can train as operators in a few months. This job is dangerous enough for professionals. You send us amateurs!' He then went on to explain the inadequacies of the broadcasting sets. The S.O.E. representatives replied that they were sorry, but after all, the needs of the Danish Resistance did not rate high priority.

Why not, Duus-Hansen suggested, let the Danes try to solve their own radio problems? He personally would undertake to recruit professional operators in Denmark, and if the British would send him frequency crystals, he would find a way to provide transmitters suitable to Danish needs.

The British were frankly sceptical, but eventually London decided to give the Danes a chance, and crystals were dispatched to Copenhagen. Within a few weeks Duus-Hansen produced one of the most remarkable pieces of gadgetry used by any Resistance organization. The wireless set he built in occupied Copenhagen was smaller than a London telephone directory, worked on both alternating and direct current, used valves that could be replaced with those in almost any Danish home wireless, transmitted on all the frequencies assigned to the Danish Resistance, weighed only three pounds, and had twice the power output of the British-built transmitters. Later, one of these sets was sent to England to be studied for possible reproduction for use in other occupied countries.

Duus-Hansen and the British agreed that, ideally, each radio operator should have three transmitters at his disposal, and a man named Ruhe agreed to make parts for about sixty in his Copenhagen factory. A post and telegraph engineer named Hasselback then studied the set with Duus-Hansen and made several suggestions, and among other things, reduced its dimensions even more. In the occupied city a clandestine assembly line began to put together the tiny sets at night.

Duus-Hansen had little trouble recruiting the promised operators, and these professionals—only one, Jens Holback, was a radio amateur—established regular powerful wireless contact directly between Britain and the Resistance cells throughout Denmark. Satisfied with the service, the British no longer bothered to train Danes to send into the country as radio operators.

Broadcasting to England was in many ways one of the most dangerous jobs in the Danish Resistance, for the Germans moved efficient direction-finder units into the country, and the Danish operators found themselves the quarry in a constant cat-and-mouse game. At least four guards were stationed in streets near where transmissions were made, to give a warning if direction-finder vans approached. Both BOPA and Holger Danske offered to destroy the vans, but the radio men thought this was a bad idea because they could be easily replaced, and, also, it was felt that the Germans in the vans would be less bothersome if they were not forced to carry on a form of open warfare. Moving from one place to another, often sending a transmitter ahead the day before a broadcast, leaving it after the transmission had ended, and then returning for it later, the operators did their jobs well, sending from country farms, from houses in busy city streets, and often from hospitals.

Direction-finders could not be enclosed in steel-bodied vehicles, but the Germans, disguising the vehicles as canvas-covered delivery vans, made the mistake of using petrol-driven vehicles at a time when all Danish transport was powered by wood-fired gas generators, petrol being unavailable to civilians. Some of the radio operators' guards learned to spot the vans nearly a mile away.

When Fischer-Holst, one of the operators, had difficulty stringing up an outdoor antenna one day, he decided to experiment with an indoor aerial. To his surprise, the British responded that his message was coming in particularly strongly. From then on the broadcasters hung their aerials indoors, thus making detection less likely.

All of the operators had many exciting experiences. Once a Jutland radio man was to transmit from a hotel where, unknown to him, the Gestapo occupied some rooms. After he had gone to bed that night there was a shattering explosion. A sabotage charge had sent the whole building up in flames. In his pyjamas, the broadcaster climbed toward the top of the hotel, the precious radio transmitter in an attaché case in his hand. From the rooftop he saw Danish firemen raising rescue ladders, and he let them take him and his attaché case down the ladder. Pretending to be dazed, he then walked straight through the German police cordon around the hotel.

During one transmission from a Hellerup villa, Fischer-Holst was warned that a director-finder crew was parked outside the house. After patiently finishing his broadcast, he stepped out of the front door. A petrol-driven van with a canvas enclosed body was at the kerb. Calmly the operator paused, plucked a rose from a bush growing at the doorway, slipped the flower into his lapel, and strolled past the Germans.

Fischer-Holst's closest call came when he broadcast from the Herlufsholm Grammar School in a manor house in Næstved, a village fifty miles south of Copenhagen. He had to tap out his message from a classroom full of wide-eyed Danish schoolboys. Just as he was signing off, one of his guards came to warn him that a direction-finder unit was near by, and that the school swarmed with Gestapo men. Not stopping to get rid of the transmitter, Fischer-Holst was led through the north

wing of the building to the chapel. He could hear German
voices outside.

The Herlufsholm Chapel, a thirteenth-century building,
is the final resting place of many famous Danes. Hiding
behind the casket of one of Denmark's most famous admirals,
the little radio operator had an idea. He slid aside the stone
casket lid and placed his radio transmitter inside. Closing the
sarcophagus again, he escaped through a side door. Minutes
later the Germans entered the chapel, and certain that the
Resistance operator was still in the building, searched it
methodically, but they never thought of opening the caskets.
Fischer-Holst, meanwhile, was able to get far away from the
school, and several days later his guards returned to retrieve
the broadcasting set.

The danger to the radio operators remained great as the
demand for their services increased. The airwaves between
Denmark and England were crowded, and the operators could
be asked to take no greater risks by transmitting more
frequent messages. Sent to Sweden to discuss with the British
the problems of more broadcasts, Duus-Hansen received the
suggestion that the Danes try using high-speed sending
equipment. Of course, the British said, they doubted that he
would be successful. Mechanical devices did exist that could
be used to send speedy messages, but the British did not see
how such equipment could be adapted to clandestine
broadcasting. They admitted frankly that none could be
spared for Denmark. Duus-Hansen, however, had some ideas.
'You set up your receivers,' he told his British friends, 'and I
believe our people can do the rest.'

In a few days the Danes had solved the problem. Stealing
equipment from a Frederiksberg officers' training school, the
Danish Resistance managed to be on the air with high-speed
transmissions four days after the British conferred with Duus-
Hansen. The messages were perforated on paper tapes which

were run at speed through a broadcasting transmitter, and the signal, sounding almost like a continuous blip, was received and recorded on ordinary gramophone discs. The records needed only to be played back slowly to transcribe the messages. As many as eight hundred letters a minute were sent this way. The messages were transmitted in a numerical sequence, and as long as no numbers were missing, the British did not bother even to send confirmation messages. Soon the Danes built tiny high-speed players, so small that one of these would fit inside an attaché case with the broadcasting sets.

As the German direction-finder vans became more of a nuisance to those operators who still had to transmit at normal speeds, Duus-Hansen was flown from Stockholm to London to discuss other possible radio techniques. In the face of German vigilance, he suggested; why not establish a Danish radio relay station in Sweden?

The British said that, officially, they could not give their permission to have Sweden's neutrality violated in this way— but such a system would nevertheless be welcome. 'Mind you, one of the British officers cautioned, 'we must forbid such action.'

The American Embassy in Stockholm agreed to establish a consular annexe in Malmø into which they would move one of three American wire recorders then in Europe, and into which Duus-Hansen would move some of his Danish-built equipment. He then assembled a relay station in the top storey of the building, and soon high-speed transmissions began on the Denmark-Sweden-Britain hook-up on ultra-high-frequency. Because the Germans were sure no secret radio would ever broadcast on such a wavelength, this signal was thought to be commercial and was not even monitored.

Some months earlier, a Mrs. Bonnesen, Duus-Hansen's code girl in Copenhagen, had been captured by the Germans and taken to Shell House for interrogation. Left alone for a few minutes, she had succeeded in walking out of the building and strolling past the guards, through Copenhagen, and to Duus-Hansen's headquarters, the only person ever to make such an easy escape from the Copenhagen Gestapo offices. In Sweden she had been appointed an American consular assistant. In this capacity she would be useful to the Resistance. A second Danish radio station was erected in Sweden, this time in the U.S. consulate in Helsingborg. Operated at first by an American and later by Mrs. Bonnesen, it received not Morse but voice messages, and it dispatched relatively low priority communications such as *Information* bulletins. These would then be sent out of Sweden through diplomatic channels. Later Mrs. Bonnesen went back to Malmø to work the relay station there, and she also received British and American airmen who had been slipped out of Denmark by the Resistance.

When the Germans began having supply problems toward the end of the war, the Danes decided to attack the direction-finder vans. Fischer-Holst was to act as decoy and Holger Danske saboteurs would blow up the Nazi vehicle when it drew near. However, the saboteurs, seeing Fischer-Holst's guards lingering near by, thought they were part of the locator's crew. By the time the guards had explained themselves, the German van was so near that all the men—guards and saboteurs alike—had to rush to warn the operator to stop his transmission. Luckily, none of the Danes was apprehended.

Another raid on a direction-finder van was slightly more successful. The van was fired on by Resistance agents and several Germans were killed, but after a short battle the van withdrew on bullet-flattened tyres. This attack so worried the Germans that afterwards they always skirted no more closely than half a mile from the transmitting places.

Early in 1945 the Danes found what was probably the final solution to their radio problem. They erected a directional sending antenna of the south coast of Sealand, opposite Malmø. Broadcasting on ultra-high-frequency, and using special reflectors that allowed broadcasts to be aimed on a slim five-degree beam, they worked undetected. From the time this system was established until the end of the war, the main purpose of other broadcasts on the conventional transmitters was to divert the Germans from this service.

Of about twenty Danish operators, only four or five were caught and killed, and these because they were lax in obeying security rules. If they were captured, the operators had been told to broadcast for the Germans, making sure to omit the coded recognition signal in the 'preamble' of their messages. Resistance radio codes were of a type that could not be broken—even if the Germans captured the charts and had the code system explained to them. One Danish operator was taken by the Gestapo and forced to send a coded message to England saying that he had forgotten the name of the Jutland sabotage leader and also the man in charge of Resistance finance. This was much too obvious a ruse, and the German message was bound to be recognized as false even had the absence of the recognition signal not alerted the British. In any case, other Resistance radio people had already signalled that one of their number had been captured.

Never badly compromised, Danish Resistance radio was more efficient than any other underground broadcasting—and it was the only clandestine broadcasting worked entirely from within an occupied country.

12

The Island

ON a summer day in 1941 the German commandant on the island of Bornholm raged in to see one of the Danish officials on the island. As the Dane rose from his desk the German roared, 'Have you seen this damned magazine?'

The official glanced at the Copenhagen weekly. 'What's wrong with it?' he asked.

'Some damned journalist has written that he's just got back from a holiday in a place in Denmark where there was no blackout, there were no occupation authorities, *and* no wartime atmosphere!'

'Really!' smiled the Dane.

'Yes, really!' the German glowered. 'And where do you suppose this paradise is? I'll tell you where it is! It's eighteen kilometres north-east of Bornholm! It's Christiansø!'

The Dane smiled but did not reply.

'Damn it!' the German continued. 'Of course there's no war on Christiansø. That island's Swedish.' He paused, for the Danish officer was still smiling. 'Christiansø *is* Swedish, isn't it?'

The Dane slowly shook his head. 'As a matter of fact, it belongs to the Admiralty and the fishermen there pay rent to the Government. They're not allowed to build new houses or tear down old ones, and in the summer artists go there. A very quaint place—' He then described Christianø and the island connected to it by a foot bridge, Frederiksø—together about sixty-four acres of Danish soil.

The German flopped down in a chair, slapped himself on the back of the neck, and said, 'Well, I'll be damned! We've got to do something about this right away.'

Several days later the Christiansø people were ordered to obey blackout restrictions and German shipping rules. Two German soldiers were stationed there, and more than a year after Copenhagen was occupied, Christiansø began to feel the war.

Bornholm's occupation history was little less extraordinary than that of Christiansø. About half as big again as the Isle of Wight, Bornholm is a part of Denmark although it lies off the south coast of Sweden. Its people visit Copenhagen on sleek liners or by the regular air services, and speak Danish with a decidedly southern Swedish accent. Rich in agriculture and fishing, dotted with well-known porcelain factories and other relatively small but prosperous industries, its clean villages are mainly clusters of low, half-timbered, pastel-painted houses with orange tile roofs. Similarly coloured tiles are used for the pavements, and the roads are of Bornholm granite. Flat and low in the south, the island has a rocky coastline and craggy hills in the north. Its granite and smoothly tarred highways weave through some of Denmark's finest scenery. Bornholm is one of those places that cannot avoid being called quaint.

Not under orders from Copenhagen, the Germans who occupied Bornholm were somewhat more lenient than their compatriots in the north. Most of their original force, which varied from two hundred to eight hundred, were sailors at two submarine stations, one on the east side of the island, one on the west. A few Wehrmacht troops patrolled the fishing ports but caused the people relatively little inconvenience. Bornholm's Gestapo chief, a former waiter, was an inept policeman, and he and his men were disliked almost as much by the German sailors as by the Danes. The island's Resistance tradition goes back to the last routing of the

Swedes in 1658, but modern Resistance there was not always
feasible.

In addition to his liaison duties, Lieutenant-Commander
Vilhelm Theodor Hassager Christiansen commanded the
Danish Bornholm Marine District, was communication
officer, and also the island's bomb disposal officer. Like most
Danes, the dark, quiet man could never say no to a request,
and he appeared to acquiesce to every German demand. Of
course, he then went on about his business, sucking on his
pipe, doing exactly as he pleased. Christiansen learned that
all German submarines refitted or overhauled in Baltic
shipyards were being sent to the two Bornholm bases for pre-
battle inspection. The waters off the island are relatively free
of vegetation, making them ideal for testing U-boat sonic
devices. Many large German naval vessels also passed
Bornholm, and Christiansen always carried a small camera
in his pocket to photograph everything German. His notes
on their shipping were sent secretly to his superiors in
Copenhagen to be forwarded to the Allies, an invaluable aid
to Allied naval intelligence.

Early in the war a Bornholm physician, H. Christian Olsen,
circulated Copenhagen Resistance newspapers on the island.
In the spring of 1943 Olsen was taken as a hostage to a Copenhagen prison where he spent several weeks with many
Resistance men and Danish officers. During those weeks Dr.
Olsen learned what he could of underground organization,
and by the time he was allowed to return to Bornholm he was
in contact with The Ring, one of the politically moderate
resistance organizing groups linked with the Freedom Council.
From Bornholm Olsen would telephone a Copenhagen number, a supposed metal factory, and ask to see a representative;
a Resistance man would then turn up on the island on the
date the physician specified.

By order from Copenhagen only a few sabotage operations took place on Bornholm. Many weapons and explosives were stored there, and once a local informer was liquidated. Only one air drop was ever attempted, but the aeroplane was observed by the Germans and had to return to Britain still loaded. Bornholm had a very small Resistance Press. The island of 46,000 people was simply too small for ordinary active resistance.

Nevertheless, Resistance transport people soon learned that Bornholm was an excellent base because refugees could be sent there safely on the liners and aeroplanes from Copenhagen, and then getting these people to Sweden was easy, for the Germans were too busy and sometimes too apathetic to patrol all the little Bornholm fishing ports. The Christiansø fishermen and that island's lighthouse keeper kept their pair of Wehrmacht guards well fed and indolent, and about eight hundred refugees, including several dozen Allied airmen, were taken from there to Sweden during the last few years of the occupation without even arousing those two Germans' suspicions. Sometimes, too, boats from the little island made a wide swing out into the Baltic, then headed back to the northern coast of Bornholm where the water is deep right up to the shoreline. In such places trees block the view of the coast from the main roads, and arms and explosives could be landed easily, disguised as butter shipments for the German Army, and sent to Sealand. Meeting these shipments in Copenhagen was easy for loyal Danes. On one voyage, however, the captain of one of the liners going between Copenhagen and Bornholm saw German officials come aboard to inspect his cargo. 'What do you have in these butter crates?' a German snapped.

'Well, this one here,' gestured the captain, grinning, 'is full of machine-guns. And that other one over there is full of ammunition.'

'Very, very funny,' the German frowned, walking on to

inspect the rest of the ship. The arms and ammunition got
through without any trouble.

During the very last days of the occupation the German
commander on Bornholm announced that he would not surrender to the Russians; he insisted on capitulating to the
British or Americans. Dr. Olsen's men learned that the Russians intended to bomb the island on the night of 6th May,
1945, the day after the Germans in the rest of Denmark
capitulated. Working quickly, the Resistance moved the
entire population of Rønne—more than 13,000 people—to
the countryside, and although the Russians bombed the
town, no Danes were hurt.

Soviet troops then landed on the island and refused to leave
it again; they said they did not want Bornholm to become a
Baltic Malta. About 7,000 Russians camped in the centre of
the island, and there was little cordiality between these troops
and the islanders. Eleven months later, in February 1946, the
Russians made a propaganda show of their departure. Their
deportment—especially considering that these were the same
Red Army soldiers who had fought recklessly across Eastern
Europe—had been all right after a Moscow order halted their
first few days of savagery, and there was only one recorded case
of illegitimate paternity on Bornholm that could be blamed on
the Russians.

One series of Resistance acts on Bornholm may conceivably
have changed the entire tide of the war in Europe. From an
anti-Nazi German officer on the island Lieutenant-Commander
Christiansen heard early in 1943 of some sort of radio-directed
flying bomb being tested in Germany. Then one day the liaison
officer was visited by a Dane, not a Bornholm man, whose
Resistance credentials were good. The two exchanged
information, and again Christiansen was told about flying
bombs. He passed all of this to his superiors in Copenhagen.

Then, several weeks later, German motor torpedo boats began landing at Bornholm. This was not unusual, but it seemed peculiar to Christiansen that the men who got off these boats were rarely sailors but almost always Luftwaffe men who would be billeted at a hotel in Rønne, and then speed around from village to village in hired cars. Yet Bornholm had no Luftwaffe station. Christiansen cautiously asked the Germans who these airmen were. What were they doing on Bornholm?

'Oh,' was the guarded answer, 'they're pilots on leave.'

But to the Danish officer these men did not appear to behave like holidaymakers, and he decided to keep an eye on them. Often, too, the airmen went out on long trips in their MTBs. Why? Again and again they returned to Bornholm—every week-end, it seemed.

Soon several Bornholm fishermen told the lieutenant-commander of some strange aeroplanes crashing into the sea south of the island. Yet no pilots or life rafts were ever found, nor were any parts of these mysterious aeroplanes ever seen afloat. Christiansen kept a careful record of these crashes, particularly trying to discover from which direction the aircraft had come. He decided they must have been launched from the German coast, from some place south-west of Bornholm, and he sent details of the crashes to Copenhagen to be relayed to the Allies. So far, the stories still seemed to be insubstantial, but Christiansen kept his eyes open.

Just after lunch on the bright, warm Sunday of 22nd August, 1943, he had a telephone call in his office in Rønne from his friend, Johannes Hansen, Bornholm's police commissioner, who had been telephoned by one of his constables that an aircraft had crashed in a field on the south-eastern part of the island.

'Do the Germans know about this?' Christiansen asked Hansen.

'Yes, we had to tell them.'

'What time did your constable call?' Christiansen then asked.

'Oh, just a little while ago. Five-past one.'

Christiansen looked at his watch. 'Look, let's drive over there quickly,' he said. 'Maybe we can beat the Germans to the spot.'

'Good,' the police chief replied. 'I told my man to stay there and keep people away from the aircraft.'

As they drove across the island Christiansen asked Hansen a few questions. 'The crew of this aeroplane—German or Allied? What sort of plane was it?'

The police commissioner shrugged. 'My man was very vague. I've already told you everything I know.'

Christiansen frowned. He liked to reach crashed aircraft before the Germans—and not only because of his position as bomb disposal officer. If the aircraft were German, he might be able to find important documents. If the aircraft were Allied he might be able to help the crew escape. He was sorry he was not going alone to examine this aircraft. What would he do if it turned out to be one of the pilotless aircraft?

At about quarter-past two the motor-car turned left off the Aakirkeby-Nexø road, drove past some farm houses, and there they saw about fifty people shuffling around in front of them on the narrow road. Bornholm people are curious, and nothing would have kept them away from whatever was in that field.

'Pedersen,' Hansen called to the policeman who was trying to keep back the crowd, 'what about survivors?'

The constable shook his head and gestured toward the wreckage. Pieces of an aircraft were in the turnip field on the right side of the road, not far from an irrigation ditch. Although smashed to bits, the machine had not burned and was quite recognizable. It was very strange, much too small to have carried a crew.

Christiansen glanced at the pasture on the left side of the

road. He guessed, from a furrow the aircraft had gouged, that it had hit in that field, bounced, torn down some of the telephone wires that had been strung along the road, then landed in the turnip field. It had come from south-south-west, and since there was practically no wind, he presumed that the aircraft had flown in on a straight course. One of the farmers corroborated this and said that the aeroplane had been flying low and whistling.

'Come on,' Christiansen said. 'Let's see what we can find out before the Germans get here.'

He crossed over into the field to fetch a long tube that had broken off the aircraft when it first hit. The farmers milling about on the road now watched curiously, for the naval officer was in the turnip field and trying to wrench a part off the aircraft. Then both he and the police commissioner were using tape measures and jotting down the dimensions of this strange aeroplane. It had a wing-span of only about fifteen feet, was about twelve feet long, they noted. Its aluminium plates were painted yellow, and all the markings were in black. The aircraft's nose seemed to be full of sand, and its fuselage was filled by two cylinders that were both wrapped in wire but had been smashed on impact.

Christiansen groped into the fuselage, hoping to find a radio receiver that controlled and directed the aircraft's flight. 'Hmm,' he mumbled to himself, 'all mechanical.' This was not the guided missile he had expected.

There was no time—much less an excuse—to get the farmers to leave. Christiansen and Hansen realized that they were going to have to take a chance.

Reaching into their pockets, they both took out cameras. Hansen had already placed Constable Pedersen next to the aircraft, to give in the photograph some idea of the proportions of this strange flying machine. Both men focused their cameras, knowing how important this photography was. The farmers were very curious but asked no questions.

'Damn!' Christiansen said, 'I had only enough film for two shots !'

'Don't worry,' Hansen assured him, 'I got six.' Constable Pedersen moved over to his superior. 'Here they come, sir,' he said, gesturing over his shoulder. A German lorry was approaching, and both Danes quickly put their cameras in their pockets. They had had only fifteen minutes alone with the aircraft.

The crowd of farmers, their faces expressionless, watched as the adjutant from the Wehrmacht camp and a Luftwaffe sergeant walked towards the two Danes. The German officer looked curiously at the twisted aircraft. 'What the hell is it?'

'I don't know,' answered Christiansen. 'We only got here a few minutes go.'

'Do you think it's some sort of toy of the Russians?' the German then asked.

'Sir,' the Luftwaffe sergeant interrupted. 'It looks definitely German to me.'

'Very curious,' the adjutant said. Then, turning to the two Danes, 'You didn't take any pictures of it, I suppose?'

This was the bad minute Christiansen expected. 'Of course not,' he answered. 'Why would we bring cameras with us?' Now he would know about the farmers. . . .

The policeman also spoke quickly. 'No, we didn't take any pictures,' he said, holding out both empty hands, and grinning. 'No cameras.'

The farmers pressed in close, still trying to get a look at the strange aircraft, but none of them said they had seen the two Danes taking photographs. Bornholm people rarely volunteered information to the Germans.

'Well,' the German officer said, 'we'll have to get this out of here. Sergeant, get it on the lorry and take it to Rønne.'

While Christiansen watched the aircraft being loaded on the lorry, he noticed that Hansen was talking quietly with Constable Pedersen, probably getting more information. When the Germans drove away with the wreckage, the two Danes got back into their car to return to Rønne. Christiansen smiled at the police commissioner. 'I hope your photographs will be all right.'

'Don't worry,' the policeman said. 'They will be.'

In Rønne they had their photographs developed, and then sat down to prepare a report. Between them, they found, they could draw a complete sketch of the aircraft. 'What do you suppose was wrong with it?' Hansen asked.

'A nut was missing from the rudder's pivoting part, and the bolt was slipping out.'

'Can you get a report on this to the right people?' Hansen asked.

Christiansen said he could. Between them they had six first-class photographs of the aircraft to accompany their sketches and notes. Christiansen's superiors in Copenhagen would take this seriously.

Police Commissioner Hansen, because he had to, made an official report, but since it would be seen by the Germans, he carefully omitted mentioning the photographs.

Christiansen sent the data and heard nothing more about it until about ten days later when the Germans on Bornholm were ordered to send him under arrest to Copenhagen. The German sailors thought this order was the result of a mix-up, possibly connected with an incident in Copenhagen. On 29th August, Danish naval officers, learning their ships were to be taken over by the Germans, had scuttled the vessels in their anchorages.

In Vester Prison in Copenhagen the Germans wasted little time being polite to the lieutenant-commander, but threw down some papers in front of him—a copy of his entire report on the mysterious aircraft. 'You said you didn't take any pictures?' one of the Germans snapped.

Christiansen nodded.

'What about these?' asked the German, slapping prints on

his desk of all six of the photographs that had been sent from Bornholm.

Christiansen would say nothing, and the Germans set about trying to get information from him in their own way.

Although one copy of Christiansen's report had been intercepted, at least one other copy reached Sweden safely and was relayed to England. Intelligence experts there took it seriously—very seriously. The painted markings on the strange little aeroplane had said, 'V1-83.' This was the first technical data London had seen on the flying bomb, and the information was very complete.

Christiansen steadfastly refused to answer questions. Eventually Resistance men in Copenhagen contrived to get him away from the Germans, and he was smuggled to Sweden, and there he did much valuable work for the free Danes. But even before he was able to get back on the job, England had acted on his report. The place south-south-west of Bornholm from which that early version of the V-1 had been launched was Peenemünde. It was severely bombed, and the Germans were held up in their V-1 programme and unable to launch their first missiles until eleven days after the Normandy landings. Lieutenant-Commander Christiansen was awarded the Distinguished Service Cross. Police Commissioner Hansen received no decoration—but perhaps he felt it sufficient reward to know that his work was responsible, equally with Christiansen's, for sparing London much devastation and its citizens untold loss and grief.

13
The Kattegat Bridge

WERNER GYBERG, a Copenhagen radio dealer, spent the first days of the occupation searching all over Denmark for organized underground contacts, only to find one of the most useful right in his own place of business. Guessing that the charwoman there might know Resistance people, Gyberg whistled *verboten* patriotic melodies or muttered anti-Nazi jokes whenever his sales rooms were being mopped. He had no idea that this would indirectly result in his leading one of the best, smallest, and most unconventional cells in the Danish Resistance. Swedish public servants would jeopardize both their jobs and their country's precarious neutrality to assist the group. Its Danish members, mostly seamen, would usually work either disguised as Swedes or in Wehrmacht uniforms.

The charwoman's husband, a seaman on the Lubeck–Copenhagen–Gothenburg–Oslo Danish freighter, introduced Gyberg to his captain, Østrup Olsen. In 1941 Olsen permitted his vessel to become a Resistance postal carrier.

Gyberg's other underground activity led to his arrest in 1942, but Captain Olsen continued hauling Resistance mail up the Sound, across the Kattegat to Gothenburg.

Friendly police soon arranged Gyberg's escape from Copenhagen's Vester Prison so that he could live and work underground in the capital, but when the Danish Government dissolved itself on 29th August, 1943, those policemen sought out the radio dealer. 'From now on,' they warned, 'if you get caught, we won't be able to help you. And all the Germans are looking for you.' They showed him a leaflet ordering his arrest. 'If you take our advice, Werner, you'll go to Sweden.'

'That's a good idea,' Gyberg replied, 'but how?'

'We've already arranged everything,' one of the policemen said.

On 4th September, in a leaky rowing-boat, Gyberg and six other refugees crossed the Sound. In Sweden the first Dane he visited was Ebbe Munck.

'Werner,' Munck said, 'as of now, consider yourself a diplomat. You're assigned to our Gothenburg consulate, and we're getting you a harbour pass. You've had something to do with Resistance shipping, and we want you to find contacts on all the Danish trawlers and coasters in the port. Captains, cooks, seamen, anybody—get them to work for us.'

Although at first Gyberg found few helpers, after the October evacuation of the Jews more of the Danish fishermen arriving in Gothenburg agreed to work for the Resistance. Mainly they smuggled bales of British propaganda material across the Sound—a very passive job. Gyberg's own tight little group was yet to be formed.

Toward the end of 1943 Munck raised 4,000 Swedish kroner with which Gyberg bought a small, forty-year-old Swedish Kattegat trawler he re-named *Dronningen* (*The Queen*). Several Danish refugee saboteurs would crew her, Gyberg decided, and just one sailor would be able to operate the ship.

Unfurling Swedish colours, *Dronningen* lurched westward from Gothenburg, her fish holds packed with propaganda leaflets. By chance she met Danish trawlermen on the fishing banks south of Læsø Island, east of Jutland, and they agreed to get the contraband into Denmark. All the saboteurs were retchingly seasick throughout the twelve-hour voyage, but luckily they encountered no German patrol boats to engage in battle.

Getting across the stormy Kattegat was never easy, especially with an inexperienced crew, and what if they met a Danish trawler with a German spy aboard? Gyberg was far from happy with the arrangements until the day a Jutland fishing boat pulled into Gothenburg. In addition to a full refugee load, she carried Albert Sabroe, a Resistance leader from Frederikshavn in Jutland. Sabroe spoke enthusiastically with Gyberg. 'I'll see to it that the trawlers you meet off Læsø are safe, and you can run regular sailings.'

'I don't know,' Gyberg replied sceptically. 'I'm supposed to be a diplomat, and you know how things are in Sweden these days. . . .'

But *Dronningen* began sailing to a timetable and officials in the Swedish port either saw—or pretended to see—nothing. Scandinavians know Gothenburg as 'Sweden's conscience'.

In April 1944, Gyberg received money to buy another old 150-ton trawler, *Marianna*; she needed a three-man crew. Later, he bought the new, 225-ton *Mercur*, a ship so speedy that her five seamen sometimes risked running up the *Dannebrog* when near Jutland. The three vessels' hefty, one-cylinder diesel engines never faltered despite scant maintenance and the Kattegat's buffeting. The saboteur crewmen, however, never became the best of sailors, and Gyberg finally replaced them with Danish fishermen. This was the Gothenburg Group.

Their problems seemed endless. British aircraft flew Denmark's guns, explosives, propaganda and other material to Stockholm, and carefully disguised, these reached Gothenburg quite easily. But how to sneak the crates into the closely guarded harbour? Making cautious inquiries, Gyberg found an easy way. The mild-mannered police officer in charge of Gothenburg's port security, Pehr Synnerman, and his assistant, Gustav Lind, lent a hand. Soon their office began to resemble a warehouse, and when things had to be moved quickly, Gothenburg's police cars were used. 'I'd hate to think what would happen if you were caught,' Gyberg said.

'I suppose,' Synnerman replied, 'we'd be at war.'

Awaiting Jutland trawlers, the Gothenburg boats fished, and

their catch went to the Jutland vessels to thwart suspicious
German guards in the Danish ports. When fish ran particularly well, the surplus was brought back to Gothenburg, sold,
and the money went into Resistance funds.

One of the most difficult problems in bridging the Kattegat
was communication, for rendezvous points had to be picked at
the last minute, and the small boats in Denmark had to know
the type and size of cargo they would receive. Yet German
radio vigilance in Denmark was great. Two ingenious codes
solved the problem—again with Swedish help.

Throughout the war the Swedish radio presented Danish-
language news bulletins, and the Radio Stockholm newsreader
received telephone calls from Gothenburg whenever one of
the Resistance trawlers neared Denmark. A few people's names
would be mentioned in the conversation—and the broadcaster
knew what they meant. Reading his next bulletin he would
then prefix a section with a few words—perhaps, 'The war'—
spoken sharply. Hearing this, the Jutland trawler-men would be
alert for their signal—perfectly concealed.

Danish broadcasters have countless ways to sign off; and the
closing of the Stockholm summary was the signal to the fishermen. Thus, 'Good-bye, good-bye; we'll be together again',
meant that *Dronningen* was to be at a certain place on a certain
day with a heavy load of weapons. Not only did the Germans
not break the code; they never realized it was being used.

One moonless night early in 1944 one of the trawlers had
eased out of Gothenburg harbour, its illegal cargo stacked
high in fish crates on the decks. The sailors did not know
that a Swede who spied for the Germans had managed to
send a message to the Nazi patrol vessels that the unarmed
trawler was coming across the Kattegat, and the German boat
located and approached the trawler. Fortunately, her
accumulators were low, and the trawler's lights barely showed.
Gyberg, standing watch on deck, heard a voice in German
call out across the water: 'Halt !'

But the Danish boat kept chugging on its course, and again a German voice shouted: 'Halt!'

'What should we do?' one of the seamen whispered to Gyberg.

'Keep going. What else *can* we do?'

'Halt!' the German shouted again, his boat now so close to the trawler that the two vessels nearly touched.

The Danes were silent.

Then one of the Germans screamed impatiently, 'All you damned Swedes think you own the whole world! But you're wrong! We're Germans—do you understand?'

Still the Danes said nothing. They were outside Swedish territorial waters now, and most of their contraband was in unsealed crates on deck.

'Halt, I said!' a German again shouted.

'You know what you can do with your orders!' one of the Danes taunted. At the same time Gyberg switched off the dim navigation lights, and in the thick night they began pulling away from the Germans. Across the water a German yelled like a small boy, 'All you damned Swedes can go to hell!'

The thick mist that draped low over the Kattegat muffled the trawler engine's *tunk-tunk-tunk*. And the more violent the Germans' curses became, the more lustily the Danes swore back. The Germans dared not shoot because they could not see the Danish ship, and in the darkness they could not be certain that this was a Resistance boat. Eventually the back-and-forth swearing stopped, and the trawlermen found that the patrol vessel either had left them or lost them in the darkness.

On the next westward voyage a German patrol craft again was waiting, pretending to be a Danish patrol ship and flying the *Dannebrog*. When this vessel challenged the trawler the Resistance seamen again kept silent, lined the rails on deck, and squinted out into the black night. The bow of the German ship nosed to within a yard of them, but the Danes remained silent. In a fight, their lack of arms would have cost them at least their boat, and probably their lives. Again the moonless night enabled them to slip away.

Another tense moment came at a time when one of the trawlers should have been already fishing out of sight of land off the Jutland coast, awaiting boats from shore to offload cargo. Gyberg was on the trawler, having left another man behind to look after the Gothenburg office, and that man was visited by one of their contact men from Frederikshavn. 'I've just had a message from the other side,' the man said. 'The Germans have found out from a Swedish Nazi where the rendezvous is going to be. You've got to call back the boat or there'll be trouble.'

'It's too late,' the other Dane replied, 'but you don't know the size of the trouble. The boat's overloaded, and there are some passengers aboard, and one is a Dane from Britain, a sabotage leader who's supposed to go down through Jutland into Germany.'

There was not time to wait for Radio Stockholm's next broadcast, and the Gothenburg Group's trawler would not be listening for such a message, anyway. 'Maybe,' the Frederikshavn man suggested, 'your Swedish friends might help.'

The Gothenburg Group man rushed frantically to Pehr Synnerman to explain the situation. Perhaps, the policeman said, a Swedish coastal patrol aeroplane could fly out and drop a message to the trawler.

The Gothenburg Swedes dispatched an aircraft, and during the next hours the two Danes waited tensely for news. But when the aircraft returned, its pilot apologized: 'We couldn't find them anywhere.'

Had the Germans sunk his boat, the Gothenburg Group man wondered. Or had she been taken into a Danish harbour and interned? Either way, this seemed to be the group's first major catastrophe.

No word came for three days, neither by radio from Denmark nor through the Swedish police. But four nights after the boat had left, the Gothenburg Group agent on his quay heard the steady *tunk-tunk* of a trawler's diesel. Through the mist he saw the outline of his ship, her decks lined by men, ease to the dock. Somehow the rendezvous had been made, and the trawler was returning unharmed with a full load of Danish refugees, all very seasick, but all very happy to see the lights of Sweden. What had happened?

Gyberg, on a hunch, altered their sailing plan, and they had returned on a southern route—much slower, but perfectly safe. He was horrified when he learned how close they had come to being caught.

All sorts of people were taken out of Denmark on the trawlers, but because it was difficult to smuggle passengers ashore in German-patrolled harbours in Jutland, only special people could be carried westward. And when Gyberg received passengers in Sweden he often had the chore of feeding and clothing them, for many of these people had fled too quickly to have time to bring along their things. When the trawlers brought Allied fliers to Gothenburg, such men had to be taken quickly to Stockholm before they were noticed, for there was always the risk that they might be interned.

No passenger fares were ever charged, of course, but when Danish banks were able to provide money for the Resistance and this money was taken to Sweden on the Gothenburg trawlers, the group was entitled to withhold ten per cent of the funds to help cover their operating expenses. Always there was a problem of book-keeping, for the group had to show where it spent every last *øre*. The group also brought clandestine mail out of Denmark. Among the letters carried in the other direction were arrival notices to families of people brought successfully to Sweden. All letters sent westward except military dispatches had to be censored before being forwarded; some refugees foolishly wrote thank-you notes to the Resistance people in Denmark who had helped them to freedom.

After the Royal Air Force bombed the Nazi headquarters in the Aarhus University, a Jutland Resistance group prepared a plaster-of-paris relief map of Jutland ten feet long, and Gyherg's seamen had to haul this unwieldly object across the Kattegat to be flown from Stockholm to England as a gift to the R.A.F.

Inward cargoes were even more varied. If a resistance leader in Denmark needed a typewriter urgently, Gyberg had to get it. Often he had to make purchases through Swedish black-marketeers, especially of such things as bicycle tyres for the Jutland people; scarce in Sweden, the tyres were unobtainable in Denmark. He bought food and clothing, chocolate and cigarettes—and even guns. Many of the automatics used by Denmark's Resistance men were bought secretly in Sweden by the Gothenberg Group, packed in fish crates, and shipped west in the trawlers.

Altogether, the trawlers carried between two and three tons of high explosives, but their tonnage of other cargo was greater. Although much of this material was either bought in Sweden or flown in from England by the British, in the winter of 1944 it came on the Moonshine ships. These were four high-speed British cargo boats designed along the lines of motor-torpedo boats, raced by Norwegian and British crews directly from Britain to Lysekil, a Swedish port near Gothenburg. Although intended primarily to get vital Swedish ball-bearings to England through the German blockade, the Moonshine ships brought heavy loads of explosives and arms for the Danish and Norwegian Resistance organizations. During the dark winter these boats each visited Lysekil several times a month. Only one of them was sunk, although all of them had many narrow escapes.

If shipping had been the only task of the Gothenburg Group, its men would have been busy enough—the entire cell comprised only about twenty men—but early in 1945 the group took on other duties. The Germans, losing heavily on every front, were tense and nervous, and Gyberg's men decided to rattle them more, so the Gothenburg Group began a psychological warfare campaign.

'Five minutes to twelve! Hitler's time has almost run out,' Allied radio propaganda broadcasters had been hammering at the Germans. Soon the German Consulate in Gothenburg began getting strange telephone calls. 'What time is it?' a voice would ask in German.

The consulate's telephone operator would glance at her watch and give the time.

'Oh, no" the voice would reply, 'it's five minutes to twelve— Hitler's time.' Then there would be a click and the telephone line would go dead. In a few weeks the Germans received several thousand such telephone calls, none of which could be traced.

Flats and houses were impossible to find in Gothenburg, but one of the local newspapers early in 1945 carried a large advertisement for a flat at a very favourable price. Hundreds of people tried to rent it. The address and telephone number of the flat were those of the German Consulate.

In the war's last days the group went into direct battle against the Germans. The Russians were pressing westward, and the Nazis planned to evacuate nearly half a million East Germans to Denmark. Since the Germans could spare none of their own boats, they decided to use Danish vessels for the move. The Danes felt that they must prevent their country from being flooded with enemy civilians, and in Copenhagen sabotage groups successfully blocked many Danish freighters in the harbour. Gyberg's men were asked to join in the action in their part of the sea.

While *Tula*, a Danish freighter on the Stettin run, was in Gothenburg, some strange cargo was gently lowered on to her deck. A large, quite ordinary looking case, it was unusual because it could be opened from inside.

Tula cleared the harbour and was beyond the shoals that protect the mouth of the Gothenburg inlet, when one of her lookouts picked out a lifeboat. Through glasses the *Tula*'s captain studied the four men in the boat and decided they must have been in the water for some time; all of them appeared to be exhausted. As *Tula* swung back her engines, the small boat rowed near, and the crew on the freighter began helping the shipwrecked men aboard. Indeed they were very sick, and the first of the men, Werner Gyberg, was shivering noticeably.

Gyberg looked nervously behind him, and as the last of his three men mounted *Tula*'s deck, drew an automatic from under his oilskins. The deck crew raised their hands, and Gyberg told his men to help Østrup Olsen and the other seaman out of the crate that had been put on *Tula*'s deck. From the bridge a message was signalled on the ship's horn to Gothenburg.

'Send a pilot out for the *Tula*?' a Swede in the harbour master's office replied. 'But we've only just cleared her.'

The reply took some time to decipher. 'Come out, anyway. *Tula*'s now under a new proprietor.'

The Danish freighter was interned in the Swedish port. Her log had an entry in Gyberg's hand explaining that the ship was the property of free Denmark.

A few days later Gyberg asked his police friend, Pehr Synnerman, for a strange favour. Several Wehrmacht soldiers, down from Norway, were being held in the Gothenburg prison, and, at Gyberg's request, Synnerman took from these men their uniforms and a large Nazi flag. Aboard the trawler *Mercur*, well out on the Kattegat, a special crew of Danish saboteurs donned the uniforms, lowered their Swedish ensign and raised the swastika.

Eventually *Mercur*'s crew, all seasick, saw a large Danish freighter, the *Lynaes*, approach. 'Signal them to heave to!'

Then the Danes in the trawler watched the familiar, ridiculous scurrying. From almost every one of the freighter's portholes papers dropped into the sea—illegal pamphlets, newspapers and other matter the Nazis would not want to find aboard a Danish ship.

The *Lynaes'* passengers and crew were startled when they were told to head back to Gothenburg, dumbfounded when they heard these Germans speak impeccable Danish. But one more freighter was kept from being used to dump unwanted Germans on Denmark.

The Gothenburg Group operated like a pirate band. Although before the end of the war more than 18,000 Danish refugee civilians and 5,000 members of the Danish Brigade were in Sweden, security rules made Gyberg's men avoid their compatriots. Werner Gyberg went on only about five of the crossings himself on the trawlers, and the trawlers altogether made about one hundred and fifty voyages. Never armed, braving the worst of seas, they got more than a thousand people safely out of Denmark without losing a passenger until the very end of the war. Then a new Danish ship the group had just bought and was using to make direct runs, changing from the *Dannebrog* to Swedish colours to land in harbours on both sides of the Kattegat, was taken by the Germans and her crew and passengers sent to a concentration camp in Denmark. But the end of the war was at hand, and within a few months they were again free men.

14

The Secretary and the Pastor

THE Gestapo had three headquarters in Denmark, one in Shell's new Copenhagen office building, a second in an agricultural college near Odense, and the third in the Aarhus University buildings in Jutland. In each were carefully guarded files of all information the Germans collected on regional Resistance activities. From each of those card indexes a picture of underground development would eventually emerge which would enable the Nazis to crush the organized Resistance. By early autumn, 1944, the Aarhus records were almost complete.

The Danes sent urgent radio messages to Baker Street for help, and Air Vice-Marshal Basil Embry took up the matter of assigning the task to Mosquito bombers whose crews were specialists at pin-point raiding. Svend Truelsen, planner of Colonel Ørum's escape, and by then a major in British Army Intelligence, and Squadron-Leader Ted Sismore, the squadron's senior navigator, were among the planners who were called in to study the intelligence material on the Aarhus University, planning a way to bomb the Gestapo buildings without harming a nearby hospital. Major Truelsen believed it could be done, and Squadron-Leader Sismore hoped he was right.

Fifty-year-old Pastor Harald Sandbæk felt the Germans had a right to end his life, but he knew no rule of warfare that allowed them to torture him. Early in the occupation he had sold illegally printed Resistance books, and in 1942 he organized about ten members of his small congregation in Hersum,

in North Jutland, to receive British air drops and to help
Allied airmen to escape. Later, when one of his friends was
captured and tortured into giving information, Germans
raided Sandbæk's home when he was out, and the pastor then
went underground, leading a small sabotage group that also
received air drops. Twice, on command from Resistance
superiors, Pastor Sandbæk ordered the liquidation of informers. On 15th September 1944 he and six of his men were
ambushed in a Jutland high school, and two days later several
more members of their group were taken.

Kept in cells in the Aarhus Prison, every day the pastor and
his men were taken to the Gestapo offices in the university
for interrogation. None ever saw the others, and none knew
what the others had been made to tell. In the beginning the
pastor had resolved to say nothing, but he was at first amazed
and later dejected at how much the Germans already knew
about him. His interrogation was hard; one session began at
nine o'clock in the morning, continued all day, through the
night, and all of the following day until midnight. 'Come
on, Sandbæk,' the Gestapo men snapped, 'twenty hours ago
you said this!'

To jog his memory, the Germans beat him with clubs and
their fists, and kicked him as he sprawled, handcuffed, on the
floor. In the end, the Germans promised, they would execute
him, and to that he became resigned, for in the beginning of
the year Nazi thugs had assassinated his friend, poet-playwright
Pastor Kaj Munk, for doing much less. But what drove Pastor
Sandbæk into a feeling of complete hopelessness was that the
Gestapo seemed to know so many of the smallest details of his
group's activities.

On 7th October, three weeks after Pastor Sandbæk was
arrested, Ruth Philipsen was sent to a meeting in Aarhus
between underground intelligence agents and a parachutist
from England. The day before, Ruth had been to the same
meeting place and had been suspicious of the people she had

met there. 'They're Gestapo agents. I'm sure of it,' she told the Danish intelligence officer she worked for. But the Resistance man said she was mistaken and insisted she go to the meeting—and there she was arrested. Taken directly to the Gestapo headquarters in the university, her interrogation began. At first she answered no questions, although the Germans knew much about her activities in Aarhus. When they asked for addresses of Resistance meeting places, she gave false ones, hoping to give her friends time to discover that she had been caught.

When the Gestapo searched Ruth's handbag, they found a doctor's prescription for iodine and sedatives. Now, she thought, they would learn everything, for although she could tell them little about the Aarhus underground intelligence people, that slip of paper established the most damning of connection—because it was signed by Dr. Ole Chievitz.

Dr. Chievitz was a well-known Copenhagen surgeon who was one of the very first Danes to resist the Germans, and not for political or personal reasons, but because he thought the Nazis were wrong. Connected with almost every Resistance activity, he was also a member of the Freedom Council. Ruth Philipsen had been his personal secretary since before the occupation, and only a month before her arrest Chievitz had sent her to join the intelligence group in Aarhus because so many of his own activities had come to light that it was no longer safe for Ruth to remain in Copenhagen. When captured, she knew the whereabouts and activities of every member of the Freedom Council.

Glancing at the prescription, the Germans said that it proved the young woman's connection with wounded saboteurs. In a demonstration of incredible stupidity, they did not notice the signature on the chit. Nevertheless, Ruth Philipsen's first interrogation lasted thirty-six hours. Her face was slapped, her hair pulled. The Gestapo put thumbscrews on her fingers and threatened to tighten them if she would not talk.

But she said nothing, and most of the threats against her were not carried out during that session.

Knowing she would have to do something to forestall future torture, the next day Ruth asked to see the Gestapo chief, Colonel Schwitzgiebel. In her soft voice she told him: 'What's happened has disappointed me very much. I always got angry when people told me that you Germans torture Danes. I always said you were a civilized and cultured people.' Then she described her interrogation.

Schwitzgiebel was full of apologies. 'My dear Miss Philipsen, I assure you, we *are* a civilized people. The men who bothered you must have been Danes. I promise you, I'll never let it happen again.'

Curiously, Schwitzgiebel lived up to his word; Ruth Philipsen suffered no more brutality, although the Germans tried everything else to induce her to give information. Once one of them asked her if she would rather be shot or sent to a concentration camp. 'Sent to a camp, of course,' she said.

'But my dear girl, you wouldn't last three weeks. Most people die there in that time.' Her interrogator then described in detail the concentration camp brutalities. 'No, if I were you, I would prefer to be shot. Really, it's the best thing.'

At other times the Germans gave her long lectures on their brand of Nordic culture, and on the upstanding character of German women as typified by their Gestapo typists. And discovering Ruth was from Schleswig, the Nazis then said in genuine astonishment, 'But then you're a German! How can you behave as badly as you do?'

To keep them away from questioning her about certain subjects, Ruth fabricated fantastic lies for the Germans. She said she was the mistress of the intelligence chief, whose name the Germans already knew. Although she was certain it could not be so, the Germans quickly told her that this officer had been captured and was badly wounded. A Gestapo man, picking up the telephone, said, 'I'll call the Military Hospital and see how your man is.

Ruth could hear the voice of the person the interrogator spoke to. It was someone on the other side of the thin wall of the room where she was being questioned.

The German shook his head. 'He'll die unless he gets special treatment right away—and he won't get it unless you tell us everything you know.'

Ruth pretended to sob. 'I tell you; I know nothing!'

The Germans tried to sustain the drama through several interrogation sessions. 'Take me to him! You must let me see him!' Ruth cried. 'Then I'll tell you everything!'

This the Gestapo agents had not anticipated, and they pretended to telephone their hospital 'I'm sorry, Miss Philipsen, but your lover has just died.'

The young secretary buried her face in her hands, sobbed and shook so much that the Germans sent her down to the dispensary in the university basement where she continued to sob. 'You must let me see his body! It's my right! Show me his body and I'll tell you anything you want to know!'

The Gestapo, considerably embarrassed, pretended to contact the Aarhus Military Hospital again. To Ruth they announced brightly. 'We were wrong. Someone else died. Your lover has escaped.'

During the next weeks, to try to make her give information, the Germans deprived Ruth of most of her food but, although she protested loudly, she had enough to keep from starving, and as she had meant to go on a diet for some time it was no great discomfort.

Then a German officer named Rosenberg, one of the men who sometimes questioned her during the day, began visiting her cell at night. He had, he said, fallen hopelessly in love with her. Ruth was non-committal. Finally, one evening Rosenberg whispered, 'I have a plan to get you out of here, and we can escape together to Sweden.' After more protestations of his affection, he added, 'But first you must tell me everything you know about the Resistence so that I can make final plans for our escape.' Ruth felt almost insulted that her captors should consider her so naïve.

The Germans had placed another woman in Ruth's cell, but the secretary, thinking that this woman might also be tortured into giving information, never disclosed any of her schemes to her. It was a wise decision, for although the woman appeared to be a Danish patriot, she was known in Resistance circles for quite another reason. A notorious informer, she had betrayed her own brother to the Gestapo for a three-thousand-kroner reward.

One day Ruth Philipsen was confronted with Pastor Sandbæk, but she did not lie when she said she did not know him. She had never met the clergyman before.

By then the pastor's feelings of complete hopelessness seldom left him. On the night of 30th October he sat in his cell with his Bible—searching for some solace or message that his reason told him he would not find. He was not always allowed to have a Bible, but that night he read it for hours. It soothed him, and gradually an idea fixed itself in his mind. *Soon you will be free.* But was not death the only freedom the Germans dangled in front of him? After closing his Bible, Pastor Sandbæk slept well.

When the Germans came to take the pastor to the university in the morning, he glanced around his cell. His only personal possession there was a photograph of his two small daughters, and on an impulse, he snatched it up and put it in his pocket. This was something he had never done before. *If I am going to be freed*, he thought, *the Gestapo mustn't use my children to force me to come back.* He shook his head. *You're a reasonable fellow, Sandbæk, but you're behaving like a madman! You're going to die here, and you know it!* But he kept the photograph in his pocket.

Driven to the university, the pastor was taken to a second-floor room for questioning by several Gestapo men. For the first time, they removed his handcuffs. On the third floor, Ruth Philipsen faced a window in a room with two Gestapo men. The two interrogations began at about the same time, and they continued all morning.

Hearing an air-raid alert just before one o'clock, Ruth's questioners told her to be glad she was not in Germany; there, they said, sirens were now almost always a harbinger of death. She did not answer. Downstairs, neither the pastor nor his inquisitors heard the siren.

Then suddenly Ruth saw a dark shadow hover over the building, and heard an aircraft engine's roar. In the next moment a blurred, silvery object streaked past the window and slammed into the next building, detonating loudly. Downstairs, the Gestapo men with the pastor ran out of the room, but the two Germans with Ruth were more calm and told her to get under a writing-table. They crouched under another table in the opposite corner, and after several bombs had hit the building, the men drew their pistols and tried to lead the young woman toward the staircase. The stairs had been demolished, so, turning back into the room, the two Germans dived under their writing-table again, and Ruth got back under the other one.

Mosquito bombers were coming over in waves, their bombs hurtling cleanly into the Gestapo buildings. One crashed through the ceiling of the third-floor room, then downward to explode on the ground floor. Pastor Sandbæk, now alone, was buried in rubble, but Ruth Philipsen was merely stunned. As the clouds of chalky dust settled, she looked across the room. The other writing-table was gone, and so were the Gestapo men. Half the floor was a jagged, dark hole. The aircraft were still swooping toward the buildings as she ran out on to a small grillwork balcony. Looking down, hardly thinking, aware only that she must get away, she climbed over the railing, and jumped. She hit on a soft grassy spot, and found she could get back on her feet. One of her stockings had laddered, but otherwise she was unhurt.

Dashing around a corner of the building, she ran toward the ring road near the university. Machine-gun fire from the aeroplanes tore at the ground around her, and she was caught in a cross-fire as anti-aircraft guns in the nearby Langelandigade Barracks barked. The only thing to do was run.

Across the broad highway she sped, then through a small garden toward some houses. Someone came out to beckon her into a basement that was full of people who had been holding a silver wedding party. At first these people stared coldly at the young woman in dusty clothes. She had not had a bath for days, her hair was uncombed, and she knew she looked frightful. But the unpleasant stares, she soon realized, were because these people thought she was from the Gestapo. When she explained that she was an escaped prisoner, the party was more solicitous, but was now afraid she might be caught with them. 'Don't worry,' she explained, 'I have somewhere to go.' Some of the guests then helped her get to an Aarhus suburb to the home of a pastor she knew quite well, a man who often helped Resistance radio people find transmission places.

A small group had gathered at the pastor's house. All in tweeds, they were about to leave for a country shooting party, and the clergyman suggested the young woman join them. Borrowing a hat and sun-glasses, she set out with the party to a suburban railway station where they were joined by others and climbed into a train.

At the University, workers were already sifting through the rubble, looking for corpses. A Resistance man who had watched the raid from a nearby building telephoned his headquarters in Aalborg, and a message was radioed from there to Britain. When the squadron that had bombed the University landed in England, they found a message awaiting them.

'BOMBING OP GESTAPO AARHUS O.K. GESTAPO HEADQUARTERS BUILDING COMPLETELY DESTROYED. ONLY ONE BOMB FAILED. LANGELANDSGADE BARRACKS IS BURNING. CONGRATULATIONS TO ALL CONCERNED. FURTHER NEWS AT NINETEEN THIRTY DANISH TIME.'

The building where Pastor Sandbæk and Ruth Philipsen had been questioned no longer stood, but several hours after the attack German soldiers dug out the clergyman. Conscious only for a moment, the pastor was asked a few questions, mumbled a reply in German, and then fainted again. He did not remember being driven to a civilian hospital in an ambulance, but when he became conscious again, a Danish nurse was at his bedside. 'My name is Pastor Sandbæk.'

The young woman was wide-eyed. 'Can it be true?'

He nodded weakly, and a Danish doctor named Buus was brought in. 'Are you really Pastor Sandbæk ?' Dr. Buus asked.

The clergyman nodded, then fainted again. The head of the Aarhus Red Cross, Børge Rasmussen, was telephoned, and he brought an ambulance to the hospital to spirit away the pastor before the Germans learned he was still alive. For several hours that ambulance cruised through Aarhus streets as Rasmussen tried to decide where the badly injured man might best be hidden.

Ruth Philipsen's shooting party alighted at a rural railway station, and was welcomed to the manor house of Count Knuth. Her clergyman friend explained that the young woman was a Miss Hansen from Copenhagen who had been living underground and had had an arduous journey to Jutland. Asking no questions, the countess led Ruth away to a bath, and lent her a change of clothing.

At five o'clock, the next radio message went to England. 'AMBULANCES WERE CARRYING GERMANS FOR SEVERAL HOURS. WE CANNOT YET GIVE NUMBER OF KILLED. IN ONE OF THE BUILDINGS FIFTEEN GESTAPO MEN HAD THEIR OFFICES. IT IS SUPPOSED THAT ALL OF THEM WERE KILLED. WE HOPE SO.'

Ruth would have preferred to go straight to bed that evening, but she was invited to dinner by the countess. Around the glittering table there was much talk of the afternoon's air-raid, and someone stated that there had been no survivors. Ruth smiled but said nothing.

Sandbæk was driven to the Aarhus Town Hall where Jens Lillelund, the Holger Danske sabotage leader, had been having a secret meeting with local people that day. The pastor, barely conscious, then had to be subjected to a final interrogation. Although he did not like to do it, Lillelund slapped the clergyman to keep him awake. 'Sandbæk, you must tell us everything the Germans know! Everything! It's important!'

After the Germans announced that the secretary and the pastor had been killed in the air-raid, the Resistance told the mothers of both people that this was not so, but obituaries for both appeared in the Danish newspapers. And Mrs. Philipsen must, Resistance men told her, request her daughter's body. The Germans said that they had not been able to find a corpse, but they returned the few things the young woman had left in her cell, and the entire Philipsen family, all except her mother unaware that Ruth was alive and in Jutland, went tearfully to the memorial service held for the young secretary in a Copenhagen church.

Six weeks after the air-raid, Pastor Sandbæk and his wife were smuggled to Sweden, and from there the clergyman was flown to England to broadcast on the B.B.C. Danish Service the first account of a wartime survivor of Gestapo torturing. On the day of Denmark's liberation, he and a Norwegian bishop officiated at a memorial service in Westminster Abbey. The Resistance had kept the Sandbæk children safely hidden in Jutland until that day.

In December, the Germans discovered that Ruth Philipsen was alive and still in Denmark, so she had to be sent secretly toward Sweden on a fishing boat. After transferring to one of the Gothenburg vessels, she was separated from the other passengers, who included two suspected informers the Danes wanted interned until after the war, a pair of Wehrmacht deserters, and eight other Danish refugees, and before the boat entered Gothenburg Harbour, Ruth was hidden under some fish nets in the hold. She had a courier bag, and the Resistance organization did not want her to waste time going through a Swedish screening camp. Instead, sometime after midnight, she was put on a rock in the harbour where she sat shivering alone until a rowing-boat came for her. She was then landed in Gothenburg with credentials identifying her as Marianna Olsen. She went directly to Stockholm.

The day after the Mosquito bombers had razed the Aarhus University buildings, a third radio message had gone to England. 'KILLED GERMANS SUPPOSED TO BE ABOUT 150 OR 165. DANES 20 OR 30. MOST OF THEM INFORMERS. SCHWITZGIEBEL KILLED. WE ARE VERY VERY THANKFUL.' The raid had wiped out an entire Gestapo headquarters and staff, and all of Pastor Sandbæk's men were released from the Aarhus Prison for lack of evidence against them.

15
The Smørrebrød Raid

LARGE-SCALE sabotage raids in Jutland were seldom feasible, although the Jutland saboteurs were no less brave or ingenious than the BOPA and Holger Danske men in Copenhagen. Some day, the Jutlanders hoped, they would find the super target—for the biggest of sabotage jobs.

One day a North Jutland Resistance man met a friend of his in the street, a machinist named Christensen, who worked for the German military. No Nazi, Christensen had been pressed into serving the invaders, and he admitted freely that he did not like it. How, he asked his Resistance friend, could he hit back at the Nazis? Could he be given some explosives so that he might sabotage the place where he worked?

The Resistance man promised he would see what could be done, and he described Christensen to Toldstrup, the underground leader in North Jutland. Toldstrup, although primarily concerned with air drops, led every sort of activity, and he immediately realized Christensen's potential value. But, Toldstrup said, the machinist must not be wasted on just an ordinary sabotage operation. Could he be induced to quit his job and then try to work elsewhere for the Germans?

Christensen agreed to go wherever he was sent, to do whatever the Resistance wanted him to do. In Aalborg, where for a long time Toldstrup had maintained his headquarters, the Resistance chief began to look for Christensen's target. The biggest German installation in that harbour city was the municipal aerodrome, then a vast Luftwaffe station. For a long time the Danes had wanted to damage it, but the field was too well guarded, and worse, no Dane was allowed to enter or leave through its gates without being thoroughly searched. Nevertheless, this, Toldstrup decided, was the place for Christensen.

The machinist found employment without trouble at the aerodrome, but when he described its layout to Resistance people, he was glum. German security on the field was just about perfect. At most, he said, he might smash a few things with a hammer, but, as far as he could see, doing large-scale damage there was just about impossible. If only there were a way to get explosives on to the airfield, things might be different, but this seemed just about impossible. He had found two other Danes who worked for the Germans on the field who would help out in any sort of sabotage action—but that only meant three hammers at work—a very small contribution.

Toldstrup and his men began to puzzle over the problem. An aerial attack against the airfield by Allied bombers would have been almost suicidal, for the installation was well protected by a radar screen, by anti-aircraft guns, and by its own fighter complement. The sort of frontal attack BOPA made in Copenhagen certainly would have been impossible; there were too many Germans stationed and alert on the field. However he considered it, Toldstrup realized, the answer was to get on the field with explosives. There had to be a way. The explosives must be camouflaged as something else— something that the workers could take on the field but would not be expected to bring out again. But what? For a large sabotage job the bulk of explosives would be great, even when divided between three men. And then Toldstrup had an idea.

There was, he realized, one obvious thing every Danish workman on the Aalborg Aerodrome took on the field every morning but did not take out at night. Toldstrup had a chat with Christensen and made a suggestion. The machinist smiled, 'It's going to be a great hardship, but we'll do it.'

Toldstrup then got men from one of his sabotage units to help in the plan. Using plastic explosives, the Resistance men began carefully preparing small bombs in the form of paper-covered parcels about eight inches square and two and a half inches thick.

Every morning Christensen and his friends each carried one of these small bombs with them past the German sentry at the gate of the airfield. The Germans never noticed a thing—for every workman on the field arrived with a similar small parcel—containing lunchtime *smørrebrød*.

Storing the bombs in the airfield was risky, but Toldstrup had suggested to the men that they do this in their clothing lockers. The biggest danger in this, of course, was that the plastic explosive had a distinctive, heady smell. But unless the Germans chanced to search the locker room, everything would be all right. Gradually the store of explosives grew until Christensen and his two friends had taken more than fifty high-explosive bombs and twenty incendiaries on to the airfield. For more than a fortnight the three men ate no lunch.

A few days after the bombardment of the Aarhus University, Toldstrup decided there were enough explosives on the Aalborg Aerodrome, and that the time for action had come. On that day, instead of just sitting down and doing nothing during their lunch break, the three Danes had plenty to keep them busy. Toldstrup had explained to them how to crush the thin copper ends of the time pencils which would arm the bombs. These delay fuzes worked chemically and were supposed to set off the bombs after twelve hours.

The day was damp and chilly, but Christensen and his two friends moved quickly and kept warm. While all the other workers on the field opened packets of *smørrebrød*, the three machinists set to work. Having filled their pockets with as many of the bombs as they could carry, they went from hangar to hangar, placing explosives in the engines or in the cockpits of aircraft and setting incendiary charges in petrol and oil storage places. One man slipped into the Luftwaffe barracks area and hid several charges carefully in one of the buildings. Another man mined the officers' mess. Their pockets empty, the three returned to their lockers for more explosives, set these in place, crushed the ends of the time pencils, and then moved on to set more charges. On the aerodrome was a mobile workshop full of very special tools brought up from Germany. The Luftwaffe were so afraid that this vehicle might be damaged in an enemy action or by sabotage that it was driven off the aerodrome every night to be hidden in a safer place. One of the three Danes managed to enter the van and place a *smørrebrød* bomb inside it.

Christensen wandered into a deserted office building with the last of his bombs. He had just concealed it, started its fuze and was about to leave when a German officer came m. 'What are you doing here?' the German asked.

'Oh, er—nothing,' replied Christensen.

'Where do you work?'

'In the machine shop.'

'Well, then,' the German asked gruffly, 'what are you doing in here? This isn't the machine shop.'

'Nothing,' Christensen insisted. 'I'd never been in here, and I was curious about it. That's all.'

'You're lying. You were up to some kind of mischief,' the German snapped, and called one of the guards to place the Dane under arrest.

By then, Christensen knew, all the bombs had been placed. They would not go off for another twelve hours.

The rest of the aerodrome staff had returned to work, and Christensen's friends were alarmed. What if Christensen talked? What would happen to them?

Both men wanted to leave the aerodrome at once, but they knew that that would be damning. The only thing to do was to get on with their work and to leave at the end of the day as if everything were all right.

Late in the afternoon, just after dark, the two men rushed in to see Toldstrup. 'Did Christensen talk?' he asked.

The two Danes shrugged.

'Were the Germans searching the aerodrome?'

The two shrugged again.

'But what happens now to us,' one of them pleaded, 'when those damned bombs begin going off?'

'Yes,' the other insisted, 'what about us? You got us into this business. Now you've got to get us out of it!'

Toldstrup agreed. They were perfectly right. In less than an hour both men had been driven by car to a fishing port. Hours before the charges were to detonate, they were out on the Kattegat, on their way to Gothenburg.

But what about Christensen? Had he talked? Were the Germans methodically searching the aerodrome for the *smørrebrød* bombs? At that time, there was no way to find out.

As the city of Aalborg settled down for the night, Toldstrup and several of his men went through the darkened streets to a house on a hill overlooking the aerodrome. From one of the top windows they studied the field through glasses. It was a very cold night, and soon the frost on the aerodrome glistened like quicksilver. At midnight, if Christensen had not been induced to talk, hell should break loose. Toldstrup and his men watched impatiently.

But at midnight nothing happened. No flashes of detonating bombs came from the aerodrome. No noises broke the night's silence. 'Maybe they're a little slow,' Toldstrup said.

Another hour passed, but all the Resistance men could see was the normal night-time Luftwaffe routine.

All night the men took turns studying the aerodrome through their field-glasses, but they saw nothing unusual. Perhaps Christensen had talked after all. Toldstrup said patiently, 'Let's wait and see what happens.'

The sun came up, and still the routine on the aerodrome seemed to be like that of any other day. If the Germans had found out anything, they had carried on their search at night, because only a few men were going about their business on the airfield. And after wrapping up all those bombs. . . .

Then, just as the Danes had decided that it was useless to watch any longer, there was a flash, a roar, and one of the aeroplanes on the field exploded, seeming to come apart in slow motion. Now the Germans were beginning to move quickly, bringing out fire-engines to put out the blaze. And then there was another blast. Another aircraft.

Toldstrup and his aides grinned at each other. So Christensen had not talked. They realized, however, that now the Germans would have more pointed questions to ask him.

On the airfield, Luftwaffe officers were shouting frantic orders. A group of men rushed up to a parked aircraft and were just going to reach into its cockpit when it blew up. Then an officer came running from a building, in his outstretched hands one of the *smørrebrød* bombs he had found. As he was running with it, the parcel exploded. And later, in the official report, the officer was put down as missing.

Ambulances began to clang out of the gates of the aerodrome. And every few minutes there was another shattering blast. The barracks went up in flame, and so did the officers' mess. In hangars and on the field aeroplanes detonated, blowing wreckage in all directions. Two hangars were completely demolished. The precious shop truck, the one filled with irreplaceable instruments, went up with a loud bang, and everything in it was destroyed.

The Germans went to Christensen and began to question him again. Was this his doing? The Dane denied knowing anything about it. He had been in that office merely out of idle curiosity, he insisted over and over again.

Several more of the bombs were discovered before they exploded, but often as not, these went off in the hands of their finders, and even if the Luftwaffe airmen had been experienced sappers they were by then too nervous to look closely for the bombs.

Smoke hung over the hangar area, and flames shot every-where. Several petrol and oil tanks were ablaze and spitting fire, and all over the field aeroplanes continued to explode. A steady movement of ambulances in and out of the field took place all day. Events, the Germans soon found, were entirely beyond their control, and they still had no idea how it had all started nor how so many explosives could have been smuggled into the aerodrome. Christensen denied knowing anything about it, and there was no way to make him talk.

Toldstrup had men keep watch on the field all day, trying to keep track of everything that had been destroyed. The explosions continued irregularly for nearly twelve hours. They had started late, the Resistance men finally realized, because the night had been so cold that the chemical action of the time pencils had been retarded.

Toldstrup's wireless operator sent a message to England detailing the success. And the reply radioed to him stated:

'. . . YOU COULD NOT HAVE MADE A BETTER ACKNOWLEDGE-MENT TO THE ROYAL AIR FORCE FOR THEIR ATTACK ON GESTAPO AARHUS.'

Christensen was sent to a concentration camp, but he never admitted having had anything to do with the sabotage operation and he was released unharmed at the end of the war. For the Jutland saboteurs the action was almost a complete triumph—the largest single sabotage action to take place in their part of Denmark—and without the loss of a single Dane.

If their glory was dimmed at all, it was because none of the three men who accomplished this mission had ever been on a sabotage operation before.

16
'Greetings to Christian'

ALLAN BLANNER had gone from Glasgow in 1933 to establish an engineering firm in Copenhagen where, in September 1939, he had volunteered for the British forces. Told to sit tight because he might be more useful in Denmark, he had had to flee to Sweden in the summer of 1943 to avoid internment. After working for a time in the British legation in Stockholm he was flown to England in the bomb bay of a Mosquito, commissioned a lieutenant in the R.N.V.R. and sent to S.O.E.'s Danish Section.

In early 1944, for the first time since the occupation, the Germans permitted Danish fishing boats to go out into the North Sea. The herring were running on the Dogger Bank, and fish were as scarce in Germany as in Denmark. S.O.E. decided that they might be able to exploit this development. Not enough arms and explosives could be parachuted into Denmark or sent on boats from Sweden, and S.O.E. had long sought a shipping link with the occupied country. A scheme to have fast boats land contraband on the Jutland coast had only been abandoned when it was shown that the Danes who unloaded these boats were likely to be compromised.

Lieutenant Blanner's first assignment with S.O.E. was to try to arrange shipping contacts between a fishing boat that would be sent from England and a boat from the fishing fleet of the south Jutland port of Esbjerg. The British Resistance contact was radioed to try to locate co-operative fishermen, and Blanner looked over interned Danish vessels in England and selected a 35-foot, single-masted vessel that could stay at sea long enough and was not likely to break down. Next he designed special cargo crates shaped like Danish fish boxes, and these were carefully stencilled with appropriate markings, and as a precaution, were seasoned with fish offal to make them smell genuine.

The Scot would go along on the small boat himself, although there would also be two captains, a Royal Navy navigation officer, a lieutenant named Davy from Lowestoft, and Tom Christensen, a Danish fishing captain. The rest of the crew, all Royal Navy, would comprise a wireless operator, a cook, and a gunner who would have a Lewis gun, the only weapon they would carry beside their pistols. The ship might as well have been lightly armed, for she would be a floating bomb.

Until that time, all explosives sent into Denmark had been packaged according to military safety precautions; detonators and high explosives were never placed in the same containers. Now Blanner appealed to his superiors to let him take the explosives packed in kits that would not have to be broken down by the saboteurs later on in Denmark. The Danes wanted all the material needed for sabotage jobs to be packed together, Blanner explained. He designed nine-inch-deep tin canisters which were about eighteen inches in diameter and would hold sixty pounds of material, and being of barely negative buoyancy, would float with their tops at surface level if they had to be pitched overboard in an emergency. When these containers were taken out of their smelly fish boxes, they would appear to have come from air-dropped containers, so that if they were intercepted, they would be less likely to alert the Germans that such things were arriving in fishing boats. The canisters would also hold broken-down Sten guns, pistols, ammunition, and booby trap devices.

The base chosen for this operation was the Northumberland port of Blyth, already being used as a secret refuelling station for the North Sea submarine patrol. Blanner went there in May 1944, and, when he received word that a fishing boat was on its way west from Denmark, he pulled down the British ensign on his little boat, and with twenty tons of arms and explosives set out for the Dogger Bank.

The sea was as calm as a lake, and except that they had only three berths and had to take turns sleeping, Blanner's men were reasonably comfortable. Their speed was slow; if they did as much as seven knots, their engine would have nearly shaken the little boat apart. After a few days' stubble had grown on their chins, the men began to look as well as feel like ordinary North Sea fishermen, and the war seemed far away.

Captain Christensen did most of the piloting because the muddy skies obscured the stars, and the Dane seemed almost to be able to smell his way toward the Outer Silver Pit, the south-east corner of the Dogger Bank, where they were to meet the Esbjerg boats. When they finally lay at sea anchor the water was so calm and the sun was so bright that Blanner took a short swim. He and his men began to grow anxious, however, when the boat from Denmark did not arrive. They started their engine, and began sweeping back and forth on the Outer Silver Pit, expecting to contact the other boat at any time. Their wireless operator received no signal from Britain saying anything had blocked the operation, so they continued their search, sometimes stopping to cast their nets in case a Luftwaffe patrol aircraft should see them.

But after five days without Seeing a single other boat, Blanner despondently knew he must give the order to return to Blyth. When he reached the S.O.E. headquarters in London to report his failure, he was told, 'Of course you missed the Esbjerg boat. She's here—in Hull.'

'What?'

'The skipper claims a German aircraft strafed him at night, and he says he was afraid to turn back to Esbjerg.'

Now Blauner would have to wait until another Danish boat could be located to off-load the Resistance material.

When they were ready to move again, Blanner felt more confident because the good weather was still holding, and Captain Christensen said the herring would be sure to be running. Certainly the Esbjerg boat would be able to come out to meet them with no difficulty.

The second night out, the sea remained treacle calm, and a soft haze settled over the water. Lieutenant Davy was unable to use his sextant, but Christensen again sniffed their way through the heavy fog toward the Outer Silver Pit. Finally the Dane announced, 'We're here,' and cut the engine. They would drift at sea anchor until the haze lifted enough for them to spot the boat they were to meet.

At six o'clock in the morning the mist wafted away, and Blanner and his men saw another Danish fishing boat not far from them. Blanner strode toward the bow and balanced himself on the gunwale, ready to jump across to the other boat when they pulled athwart it. But there was no sign from the Danish ship.

And then the Englishmen realized that the crew of the Danish boat were asleep. Christensen spoke up. 'That's not the boat we're looking for.'

The mist was almost gone, and Blanner looked around. In the half-light he now saw what seemed to be the entire Esbjerg fishing fleet, all anchored near by. Whether they wanted to or not, the Englishmen would now have to fish, drifting back and forth, hoping somehow to make connection with the right boat. Because only Blanner and Christensen spoke Danish, they wisely decided to keep away from the other vessels; even though most of these Danes could have been trusted, nothing must be done that would give away the mission.

After three days without being able to find the ship they were looking for, they radioed to have the Royal Air Force fly a spotter aircraft over the Esbjerg fleet, but the aeroplane could not pick out the correct boat, much less direct Blanner and his men toward her, and finally a wireless message recalled them to Blyth.

This time, as Blanner later learned, the operation had been spoiled by a punctured bicycle tyre. The captain of the boat they were to meet was unable to sail on time because his bicycle broke down, and he had, in fact, only managed to reach the Outer Silver Pit the day after Blanner returned to port.

Meetings between Esbjerg boats and the boats from England were simply unfeasible if timing was to be so inexact, and the men at S.O.E. studied a map of Denmark, groping for a new idea. If, they decided, a Danish ship were to set out from the Thyborøn Canal at the mouth of Limfjord in north-west Jutland at precisely the same time as Blanner left Blyth, the two boats should arrive forty-eight hours later on the Outer Silver Pit. If both boats received the same sailing instructions, there could be no slip-up.

Word was sent to Denmark to set up this scheme, and a boat was told to be at the mouth of the fjord when the B.B.C. Danish New Service's announcer read the signal, 'Greetings to Christian.' The Danish boat would radio a snap signal, a pre-selected number that would mean that she was ready. Then when the B.B.C. sent greetings to Marianne, the two boats should set out to meet at the rendezvous point in forty-eight hours. If, however, the greetings were sent to Annette, the Danish boat was to go as quickly as she could toward Hull, because this signal would mean that the Germans had detected the scheme. A fourth signal was arranged that could cancel the operation.

In the cabin of their little boat, Blanner and his men huddled around their wireless receiver at Blyth until they heard, 'Greetings to Christian', then more faintly and on a short wave band, the snap signal. The greetings to Marianne were answered by another snap signal. 'Third time lucky—maybe,' Blanner said, and again his little boat threaded through the minefield off Blyth and chugged toward the Outer Silver Pit.

Forty-eight hours later the two boats met according to plan, and the twenty tons of cargo were moved on to the Danish ship along with personal gifts to the fishermen. 'These clothes are all unmarked and perfectly safe,' Blanner explained, 'but, for God's sake, don't smoke these fags on shore! They're real tobacco—the kind you haven't had in Denmark for years.' The scent of Virginia tobacco is conspicuous in a country where only tobacco substitutes are available.

Blanner's warning, however, was forgotten by the deck boy on the Danish fishing boat and a little while later he made the mistake of lighting up on a bus. His captain barely had time to get his crew out of Denmark before the Germans came looking for the boat. She arrived in England three weeks after the meeting with Blanner, and the next trips had to be delayed until other reception boats could be found on the Danish side. And now there would be more risks, for the Germans probably suspected that there were meetings in the North Sea.

Eventually shipments began going through, although strange events sometimes halted the operations. Once the boat that was supposed to meet the Blyth vessel was cruising off Denmark along with many other fishing boats when she heard the signal, 'Greetings to Christian.' She began to steer northward toward the Thyborøn opening into Limfjord. But she was followed by all the other boats in the fleet because their captains were quite certain that the men on this one boat must have detected fish running somewhere northward. Desperate, the boat had to turn back and await the following night's sailing order from the B.B.C. The greeting to Christian was read every night for five nights, but the boat always found herself followed by the rest of the fleet. Finally, very impatient, the B.B.C. announcer called, 'Christian, where are you?' And still the boat was in no position to return the snap signal.

Inevitably Blanner and his men had some narrow escapes themselves. After being spotted by a low-flying Luftwaffe patrol aircraft on one mission, the Scot asked the Admiralty for more guns for his boat. 'We could have bagged that Jerry,' he insisted.

Cautiously the Admiralty advised him that his job was to deliver cargo, not to fight a private war from the decks of a boat which a single bullet could send sky high.

Another time, Blanner's men were returning to Blyth after a successful cargo transfer. The weather was so bad that they had to lay offshore for several days before entering harbour. Just outside the minefield's inlet they saw a Danish fishing boat hauling in her nets. If he were now to take his craft through the minefield, Blanner knew, he would disclose to the Danes on the other boat that there was something very unusual about his vessel. He knew, too, that some Danish fishing boats were forced to carry German observers aboard, and this could have been such a boat. Yet Blanner could not risk taking his vessel into any other port. 'Head toward that boat, Davy,' the Scot ordered. 'We're going to make her a prize of war.'

Lieutenant Davy grinned. 'Boarding party, eh?'

'Party of one,' replied Blanner. 'I can speak Danish, remember. I'll take her by myself.'

Feeling like Captain Hornblower, Blanner drew his pistol as he leapt across to the deck of the other boat. But he landed on a pile of fish on the deck, stumbled and pitched forward. On his feet again and brushing fish scales off his face and clothes, he explained to the surprised Danes that they would not be going home until the war was over, that their boat was to be taken into Blyth and interned. After he told them why, they came willingly, and he assured them that word of their fate would be radioed to Denmark.

Although the boats were too crowded to carry passengers, on one voyage three men were taken to Denmark for what was almost one of the most spectacular unconventional operations of the war.

The officers of the Danish Section of S.O.E. saw demonstrations of every new and unconventional weapon, and when they saw frogman gear, they decided Denmark might well be the place for an underwater operation. An intelligence report from Copenhagen soon suggested the most likely of targets.

The Langelinie is a quay on the west side of the mouth of the city's main harbour, and Danes stroll there on Sundays, pass the famous statue of the little mermaid, and look at the foreign ships that are often tied along the quay. In peacetime nearly every navy in the world has tied at that pier, for the water is deep enough for battleships. During the later days of the occupation four German warships lay along the Langelinie, an intimidation to Copenhageners. Why not blow these ships up?

Had Resistance saboteurs decided to attack the ships, they probably would have planned the raid on paper, used make-shift gear, and struck in whatever way seemed possible. But because the planners in England wanted this raid to be perfect, everything about the action would have to be foolproof, and it would have to be fully rehearsed.

Danes in British uniform at S.O.E. were asked to volunteer for the action. They could not, of course, be told exactly what they were going to do or where they would do it, and they were told that failure meant great discomfort, a likelihood of capture, and perhaps, death. From the many volunteers three men were chosen, an artist named Holm Hedegaard, a young man named Rider, and another named Christensen.

When the Royal Navy decided that the three were proficient with frogman gear, S.O.E. decided to build a full-scale layout of the Langelinie harbour in London. Since the water along the Langelinie is a little wider than the Thames as it flows through London, and since the operation could not be rehearsed in a place that could not be guarded, a training site was difficult to find. Eventually Staines Reservoir was chosen. Along one side of the reservoir the positions of the four German ships were carefully indicated. Buoys were then placed out in the water at the same positions as the buoys that mark the Langelinie channel. The operational plan called for the men to go into a house on the east side of the channel where they would don their gear and then swim under the water to the buoys. There they would come up for air and for a rest, then swim toward the four German ships, place limpet mines on each, return to the buoys for another pause, and swim back to the house on the far side of the water.

Guiding themselves only by compasses, the three young men became so adept at the operation that they could complete it in ninety minutes at Staines, and they practised it three times each day until they could run through it without a slip. When the men were ready, they were sent to Blyth with Lieutenant Blanner, who was to get them into Denmark. They were supposed to be in Copenhagen in October of 1944 for the attack.

Blanner's small fishing boat sailed out of Blyth with the three Danish frogmen aboard. Forty-eight hours later they met a Jutland boat, transhipped twenty tons of explosives, and explained to the fishermen that they had some passengers and some unusual extra cargo. 'It's not going to be easy,' one of the fishermen said. 'The Germans keep a pretty close eye on us when we come in.'

Blanner suggested to the fishermen how the frogmen could be smuggled ashore, and then he headed back to Blyth.

Before the small fishing boat pulled into the Danish harbour all three frogmen climbed into their black rubber diving suits and put on their helmets and face pieces. They were then helped to lower themselves into the fish hold. The compartment was full of fish, already iced, but the three Danes nestled down into the Wet cargo until only their chins were above the fish. There they would have to remain for many hours. If the Germans chanced to inspect the boat, they assured the fishermen, they would duck their heads below the surface of the iced fish.

The boat went into her harbour and was not inspected, and

the three frogmen, by then nearly as cold as the fish around them, had to be lifted out of their hiding place to be sneaked ashore.

When the three arrived in Copenhagen, having carried their gear with them from Jutland, they reported to the British contact in the capital. 'Are the German ships still along the Langelime?'

'Well—yes, they are. But there's been a slight change of plan.' At the last minute S.O.E. had been advised that, if the four ships were destroyed in a sabotage action, the Germans were likely to take reprisal actions against the city. But if they wanted to, the frogmen were told, they would be helped to take their equipment back to Jutland where they might find German ships to attack in one of the harbours there. None of the three was trained to plan such actions, but they agreed that they would try something.

In Aarhus, Holm Hedegaard, the artist, selected a vessel in the harbour that he thought he might be able to destroy. The other two frogmen helped Hedegaard put on his suit in a house near the water, slipped him into the harbour, and he swam toward what he hoped would be his prey. And despite the scantiness of planning, he reached the ship. Just as he was getting the limpet mine ready to attach he heard a German guard on deck call out, 'Halt!'

Hedegaard did not know exactly what to do. This was one of the things for which he had not planned. But escaping with the mine was certainly impossible, and so he let it slip out of his hands and sink. He heard splashes in the water around him, then realized that the guard on the ship was leaning over and firing a rifle. Hedegaard raised his head high as he tread water. He had to see which way to go. A moment later a bullet tore away his face mask. Miraculously uninjured, he dived beneath the surface and swam for his life.

Hedegaard and his two companions were absorbed into the Resistance, and no more Danish frogmen or other passengers were sent out from England on the Blyth boat, but she continued to make runs whenever she could. Altogether she made five contacts with Danish fishing boats, handling some twenty tons of badly needed explosives and weapons each time. Compared to the 'Shetland Bus' in Norway, this was perhaps a minor operation, but its success should be considered in the light of the fact that no men were lost on any of the contacts, that none of the Danish boats landing the contraband was ever intercepted, and all of the material was put to good use. Perhaps the meetings on the Outer Silver Pit may have given rise to a story that was popular in Esbjerg during the last days of the occupation.

According to that story, a fisherman was sitting on the Esbjerg quay reading a copy of *The Times* when a Wehrmacht officer strolled past, noticed the newspaper, kept walking, then stopped abruptly, turned, and snarled, 'Where did you get *that* newspaper?'

The fisherman was said to be very frightened. 'Oh, er—you see—' he tried to explain. 'I'm a subscriber.'

17
The Battle of Jutland

AFTER the Normany landings, when the Allied eastward push began, the Germans began withdrawing their best troops from Scandinavia toward the Western Front. From Denmark alone, a German infantry division, an armoured division, and part of a division of Russian volunteers were transferred from occupation duty to oppose the Americans and British. These troops, intelligence reports from Norway and Denmark suggested, would be followed in the beginning of November by more than a dozen first-rate divisions that had until then been hopelessly trying to fight down the Norwegian Resistance. The Germans would come by ship to Frederikshavn in North Jutland, and then be sent by train down to the Western Front. Soon, for the first time, the work of the Danish Resistance might have a strong, direct bearing on the entire war in Western Europe.

Small teams of young Danish saboteurs in Jutland had already been damaging German troopships, as well as military railways and mustering points. From now on their operations would have to become more frequent, and much more systematized— and in the autumn, as the Allies fought toward the Ardennes, the Jutlanders set to work. About three hundred young saboteurs would try to bottle up all the Wehrmacht troops that were then in Scandinavia. A very tall order.

Toldstrup, the North Jutland Resistance leader, had his men set about to establish contact with every loyal Dane employed by the state railway in that part of Denmark. Soon there was someone on every station who could be counted on to help the Resistance. Toldstrup's men now kept the port area of Frederikshavn under close watch—and word would be sent to the Resistance headquarters in Aalborg as soon as German troopships entered the harbour. As soon as the troops began to board their trains, a telephone call would be made to a railway station somewhere south of Frederikshavn. The telephones, of course, were likely to be tapped by the Germans—but Toldstrup had not overlooked this.

'Ferdinand will send you a packet of cigarettes in three days,' a Resistance man would telephone, and the loyal Dane on the station who received the call would know that it meant that a German troop train was due to pass in three hours. The railway employee would rush to notify the nearest sabotage group, and on bicycles or on foot, the young Danes would then move out, usually carrying their bulky explosives in rucksacks, to blow out a section of railway line and stop the train. Later, when the track had been repaired and the train moved on, the saboteurs would telephone to a contact farther along the line, again announcing that 'Ferdinand' would be doing something in a certain number of days, and another sabotage group would be alerted into action. 'Ferdinand' always got results, and no German trains moved undamaged through North Jutland.

The German High Command, watching the slow progress of their troops through Denmark, ordered that the most strict measures be taken. Captured saboteurs, the Wehrmacht ordered, would be made to ride as hostages in German troop trains passing through Jutland. As soon as a train was halted by a sabotage action, the young patriots would be hauled out and executed then and there. This, the Resistance soon realized, was no idle threat; one of the captured saboteurs managed to escape from a derailed train in Jutland, and he told Toldstrup's men why he had been travelling with the Germans. And at least one Danish public figure was also made to ride as hostage in the troop trains.

Now, the Resistance men decided, if they set up fuzed

charges which would not detonate until the trains passed over them, it would be possible for the saboteurs to be far away when the explosions took place. Capture then would be less likely. This also would destroy more German rolling stock, too, as well as lengths of track. Then, as they became more experienced and watched the repair crew at work, the Jutlanders began sabotaging trains as they passed through gorges or other places where repairs were hardest to make. Pulling a derailed locomotive out of a narrow gorge could take days.

The saboteurs then began destroying water towers along the lines, thus slowing down those trains that did get through. And they blew up so many switching points that the Germans had to begin a system of cannibalization, moving railway equipment from branch lines to main lines—sometimes having even to transfer long sections of track—to get their trains through. 'Ferdinand' was a very busy fellow indeed.

The Germans, following frantic orders, tried everything to keep the railway lines open. Road blocks all over North Jutland made movement difficult for the small bands of saboteurs. Motor-cars, the Germans ordered, now must not be used between three o'clock in the afternoon and eight in the morning, and many cars were halted on the roads and confiscated. German patrols lurked everywhere, but fortunately, the young Danes knew their own secondary roads well and usually they were able to cycle around the German road blocks, trudging across the fields and through woods when all other routes were cut. But it was never very easy.

The north Jutland blacksmith who stored explosives openly in his shop cycled along a country road one night toward a railway sabotage operation, his large knapsack full of explosives and detonators. Ahead he saw German troops barring the road. If he turned and tried to go the other way now, they would shoot at him. But if he were stopped and searched, he would also probably be shot. And even if he tried shooting his way through the road block, his chances of escape would be slim. So the blacksmith decided to keep on going, and as he neared the Germans, he began shouting and burbling at the top of his lungs—the bawdiest song he knew. Then, unsteadily, he veered his bicycle from one side of the road to the other. When the Germans shone their torches in his face, he grinned foolishly, drooling a little. 'Drunk as a lord!' one of the military policemen laughed, waving the Dane past.

Many other Resistance men, less quick thinking, were caught and searched. Several saboteurs, making their way along a road late one night, were halted by a Wehrmacht patrol. One of the Danes carried under his arm a large, neatly tied, white-paper parcel full of explosives. 'Raise your hands!' the German soldiers ordered before the saboteur could throw away his parcel.

Without hesitating, the Dane reached up both arms, balancing the parcel of explosives over his head. Cautiously the Germans moved toward the man to begin patting his pockets, and then his arms and legs, searching for concealed weapons. The Dane, very nervous, shivered but said nothing. Finally he was told to move along—without even being asked what was in his parcel!

After sabotage on the railway lines from Frederikshavn had made the movement of almost any troop trains impossible, the Germans began landing their transports farther south, at Aarhus, and other groups of saboteurs quickly set to work on the railway lines there. Instead of using Toldstrup's 'Ferdinand' system, however, these men radioed coded messages to England. Then, on the B.B.C. Danish Service, instructions were given to the saboteurs south of Aarhus, telling them where to strike. This system was used because there were not enough contacts on the railway stations in that part of Jutland to rely on telephones—but it was a slow and imperfect system. After an entire German division managed to land at Aarhus and then get down through Jutland in only four days, London scolded the Danes, and the saboteurs in Aarhus set to work tightening their communications system.

Soon, however, sufficient railway lines were repaired in the north, and the Germans resumed the use of Frederikshavn as a disembarkation port. 'Ferdinand' went back to work, and the movement through Denmark of the divisions from Norway remained dreadfully slow.

That winter, snow began falling early in Jutland, but if the Germans thought it would be easier to locate Danish saboteurs in the white countryside, they were wrong. By late autumn the situation had become so desperate for the Germans that they had guards, usually in pairs, stationed at fifty- and one-hundred-yard intervals along every railway line they used in Jutland. Many of the Danish saboteurs began fashioning snow capes from parachutes that had been attached to containers dropped into the country by the Allies. Now, often on skis, the young Danes moved silently to place their explosives, often within whispering distance of the tense German guards. At least once the silent, white-caped saboteurs were noticed by old ladies who afterwards swore they had seen ghosts. For the young Jutlanders the dangerous work became a sort of game—as much fun as the winter sports they had enjoyed before the war.

There were times, however, when the snow did hinder the saboteurs. One group went out and found that they could not locate the railway line they had been ordered to mine. The tracks were completely covered in snow, so the saboteurs decided to go to the nearest farm to borrow shovels. They then trudged toward the railway line in broad daylight, and in full sight of a patrol of armed Germans. Pretending to be a railway repair crew, several of the young Danes busily shovelled away snow from the tracks. Several more of the men then crawled forward and, using the banked snow to conceal themselves from the Germans, placed plastic explosives on the tracks. When this was done and the men had crawled away, the saboteurs with the shovels put enough snow over the mines to keep the German patrol from seeing the booby traps when they walked past. The next train to come through was blown up according to plan.

In other ways the snow could be a help. It was impossible for such relatively small numbers of saboteurs to be everywhere at once, but they wanted to make the Germans think they were even more effective than they appeared to be. So Toldstrup's headquarters sent a radio request to England at the beginning of February 1945. Soon the B.B.C. Danish Service began to broadcast warnings. Danish saboteurs, the B.B.C. said, were worried because a recent snowfall had covered all the mines on the railway lines between the port of Aalborg and the Randers terminus, some distance away. Now, the radio warning stated, the Danes could find none of their own charges. Before any more German trams dared move along the Aalborg–Randers route, German sappers on foot had laboriously to check the entire line, and for some days troop movements were completely held up.

By January 1945 the attacks were so impeding the Germans that no Danes were allowed to approach a water tower or pumping installation near the railways unless accompanied by German guards. Nevertheless, the towers continued to be blown up. That month even the German commanders in Denmark were reported to have admitted among themselves that the railway sabotage in Jutland might finally lose the war for the Reich. That month, also, the Danes did not confine railway sabotage to these small actions along the lines. A group of Resistance men one night fought their way into one Jutland aerodrome where the Germans were building hangers. A night exercise was then being held on the field, and the Germans there were using searchlight batteries. But the Danes moved swiftly, and soon they had blown up several locomotives attached to trains that had taken ballast to the Germans at work on the aerodrome. For good measure, before they retreated, the saboteurs also blew up six excavating machines in use on the airfield.

At the end of January, a group of about twenty saboteurs entered the Randers railway station, pistols drawn, and gathered together all the railway employees and the German guards in the station. While these men were being held prisoner, explosions began to occur all over the Randers goods yard—fifteen explosions altogether—and several troop trains, most of which were carrying Wehrmacht soldiers returning from leave, could not pass through for twenty-four hours.

The Russian push west, as well as Allied bombardment, caused the Germans a serious coal shortage which was soon felt on the Danish railways. Coal supplies were requisitioned by the Germans from Holland and from civilian sources in Denmark, some of which would be used on the Jutland railways, others in Norway where trains were also moving too slowly to satisfy the Germans. But little of this coal ever got through, for the Danes soon systematically sabotaged coal ships and the trains that were to bring the coal into Jutland.

By February 1945 there was complete chaos on the Jutland railways. Everywhere the Germans were trying to trap the saboteurs. When they had to move great distances, the young Danes had to ride on the trains themselves, and now the Germans were holding up the civilian railways to check passengers' credentials. Many saboteurs were caught this way—but in spite of this the sabotage went on.

German patience in Jutland was at an end. When, toward the end of February, the saboteurs learned that the train of General Lindemann, then the commanding officer of all German forces in Denmark, was to come through Jutland, they decided to destroy his train. They set to work carefully, and two carriages and a sleeping car were entirely demolished. One of these was for Lindemann's personal use, but unfortunately he was not in it when the charges detonated. Stepping off the train, the general excitedly screamed an order to his soldiers—which they carried out at once. They set fire to the nearest farm, and the home of a quite innocent Dane was destroyed.

Many saboteurs were killed, and many more were captured, but the Jutland railway sabotage operations—which numbered thousands—may have been Denmark's strongest direct contribution to the victory in Europe. Certainly, the Danes did nothing that had a greater strategic effect on the war.

General Montgomery, asked about the sabotage when he visited Denmark shortly after the liberation, said it had changed the entire tide of the Battle of the Ardennes. During the worst two weeks of that campaign, when Allied troops seemed likely to be pushed far back if the Germans could get reinforcements to their front, the Jutland saboteurs worked so efficiently that, for a fortnight, every train was stopped.

18
The Men in the Attic

L ATE in the spring of 1944, having outgrown Dagmarhus, in the Copenhagen Town Hall Square, the Gestapo took over the Shell Petroleum Company's modern office building in the centre of the city.

Shell House, beside one of Copenhagen's lakes, quickly became an infamous place. Dr. Hoffmann, Denmark's Gestapo chief, Dr. Bunke, the efficient compiler of the list of Danish Jews, and many other of the more sinister members of the occupation force were given office space there. Desks were put in the cellar for about half a dozen Danish Nazis who, under the supervision of a former Danish Army captain named Møller, laboured all day at translations of Resistance newspapers and other material the Gestapo intercepted. In another basement room, loyal Danes were sometimes tortured to death. The ground floor and the next two storeys became vast records rooms, and above were offices. Only the sixth storey was empty, because it lacked a heating system, and the severe rake of its tiled roof made it cramped.

After the Royal Air Force destroyed the Aarhus University Gestapo buildings, the Germans in Copenhagen became worried. Would Shell House now be bombed? How could this be prevented?

Relying on the ability of the Resistance to learn and report every Nazi move to England, the Gestapo quickly conceived a scheme, and workmen set up flimsy concrete-block partitions to make the attic of the Gestapo headquarters into a prison. Within a week there were twenty-two small cells—five along the building's west side, facing the lake, on the left arm of the U, and the others on both sides of a corridor along the front, on the U's bottom. The cells' wooden doors were plywood faced, each with five one-inch ventilation holes drilled in the top and bottom, each with a Judas window covered with a wooden flap. Each cell contained a cot, a small stool, and practically nothing else. Another six cells, quite similar, but without cots, were also built in the attic for prisoners awaiting interrogation.

Along the front hallway the Germans also put three toilets and a washroom with a mirror above each of its six sinks. There was a kitchen for the prisoners' food.

On 11th November, before the electric heating had been installed, the first six Danes were transferred from Vester Prison to the attic. Warned they would be shot if they attempted to contact each other through the small holes that had been left for electric wiring between the cells, the prisoners nevertheless whispered from cell to cell. Taken to the lavatory whenever they wished, the Danes hid messages behind the washroom mirrors—notes explaining what questions had been asked during the interrogation sessions, and what answers had been given. A Danish charwoman named Emma smuggled letters past the S.S. guards for the prisoners, and they were at first in day-to-day touch with the Resistance organization. But when Emma was caught by the Germans and sent to a concentration camp, the prisoners had to tidy up the small cell block themselves. Even after Emma was taken away, they managed to keep abreast of the progress of the war. Their only comfort was to follow news of the Allied push along a five-hundred-mile front, for all of these Danes were being tortured, and, in the end, all expected to face firing squads.

The cells were chilly, and hourly through the night the Germans turned on the lights and peered through the Judas windows to make sure the prisoners were behaving themselves. Despite this watchfulness, the prisoners learned to stand on tip-toe on their stools to squint through the cell doors' ventilation holes to see what was happening in the corridors, and later, how to push aside the flaps on the Judas windows to look out.

The Shell House prisoners, the Germans had decided, must be the Resistance *élite*, and after a second group was brought in during December, the attic housed, among others, a Danish admiral named Hammerich, and Mogens Fog and Aage Schoch, both members of the Freedom Council. If Shell House were destroyed, the Germans were by then quite certain, these loyal Danes would be destroyed with it.

The Gestapo's raids on organized resistance were increasing, and the records on the lower floors of Shell House now swelled rapidly. In December 1944 Copenhagen's Resistance radio contacted England. In line with Hitler's latest policy to 'fight terror with terror', it seemed likely that all the hostages in Shell House would be executed, anyway, so would the Royal Air Force please destroy the records in Copenhagen's Gestapo headquarters?

This request was relayed to the Air Ministry, but when they had been told of the Danes in the attic, the Ministry would sanction no such bombing. But those men in England whose job it was to be in touch with the Danish Resistance asked Copenhagen for all intelligence data on Shell House to be sent to Baker Street—just in case.

As usual, the Danes outdid themselves, and sent London complete architect's plans of the building, full details of its construction, and a statement of precisely what every room in the building was being used for by the Germans. All available photographs of Shell House were also dispatched, as well as a map of the surrounding area indicating the positions of other German office buildings, the use of buildings the Germans had not yet requisitioned, the placement of all German radar, anti-aircraft, and direction-finder units in the city, including those on the cruiser *Nürnberg*, then in the Copenhagen harbour, and even notes of the colours of all rooftops near Shell House.

Embry's planners, assisted by Danish Major Truelsen, were given all of this material and instructed to plan a raid which, they felt at the time, would never be allowed to take place. Always there was that awful human consideration—the loyal Danes penned up in the attic.

In only a week, working from aerial photographs, from maps, and from material gleaned through questioning Danes who had recently been in Copenhagen, a scale model of the centre of the city was completed by R.A.F. model-makers. Photographs of this model would show the fliers exactly what to look for.

Again and again the Resistance radio pleaded to England for a bombing, but the Air Ministry remained adamant. Fliers competent enough to hit Shell House, it was explained, had plenty of work to do in Operation Overlord, and if for no other reason than this, Copenhagen's Gestapo headquarters could not be bombed. In any case adverse weather made an immediate attack impossible.

The plans for the raid became more and more detailed, but new problems constantly presented themselves. When Squadron-Leader Ted Sismore looked over the material, he remarked to Major Truelsen, 'I don't see how it can be done. One Copenhagen street looks just like another—and all the buildings look exactly alike.'

'Not quite alike,' smiled Truelsen. 'This time the Germans have helped us. They've camouflaged Shell House, and it's now the only building in Copenhagen painted with bold brown and green stripes.'

One day Sismore remarked to Truelsen that the raid would be easier if he could show his squadron's navigators a photo-graph of the building taken from a certain Copenhagen street corner. Sismore indicated the corner, a quarter of a mile away from the proposed target. Eight days later the wanted photograph arrived from Denmark via Ebbe Munck's office in Stockholm.

The planners now grew enthusiastic, for, despite the raid's problems, they had never worked on a plan in which they had been given so much intelligence material. But still the Air Ministry seemed to bide its time; weather conditions were still too unfavourable.

On 23rd February, the Gestapo swooped down on the Copenhagen telephone exchange to try to trap those Danes who tapped German telephone lines and who warned Resistance people when their telephones were being spied upon by the Germans. A Dane, Ove Kampmann, caught the next day as a result of this raid, was taken to Shell House for questioning because the Gestapo were fairly certain that he knew where top-level daily Resistance meetings were being held.

Not only did Kampmann know about the meetings, but he was also one of the people who attended them. It was vital, he realized, that he say nothing, and he answered no questions, even though the Germans did everything they thought might make him talk. His only chance, he decided, was to bluff the Gestapo until late Monday morning—for if he did not show up at the Resistance meeting then, his friends would know that he had been arrested, and they would change their meeting-places.

On Monday morning, when his questioning began anew, Kampmann said nothing. On the wall of the Gestapo office was a large clock, and from time to time he glanced at it, noticing the painfully slow progress of its hands, hoping that the Gestapo would do nothing that would force information from him until it was time to talk. The meeting of his Resistance colleagues would end at nine. By ten o'clock he could talk.

The Germans beat Kampmann, but he kept silent as the clock ticked on. Then, precisely at ten o'clock, he spoke up:

'You'll find all of them in the Technical High School.'

'All of who?' the Germans asked.

'The heads of the Resistance. I don't know their names, but that's where they meet every morning.'

One of the Nazis, grinned broadly. 'Thank you very much,' he said, languidly rising from the chair he had straddled. He walked over to the wall, swung open the glass cover on the clock, and reached up to move its hands—back two hours to eight o'clock.

In the raid that followed, more Resistance leaders were captured, including Professor Brandt Rehberg, a prominent physiologist who was a key man of the organization, and also another man who headed the underground army that awaited Allied orders to emerge and give battle to the Germans.

Again a plea was radioed to England that Shell House be bombed, but again the British were not ready to attack.

A few months earlier, when the Bornholm–Copenhagen liner was on its northward voyage, it had passed as usual through a channel along the Swedish coast. There, as usual, all passengers were sealed below decks before the Swedish pilot came aboard. With the pilot was a tall dark man who sometimes was known as Major Lund. Lund entered the captain's cabin where another man, the major's size and build, waited. The two greeted each other, took off and exchanged their outer clothing, and then certain of their credentials. Lund remained in the captain's cabin when the ship emerged from Swedish waters, and the other man departed with the pilot. Lund did not leave the captain's cabin until Copenhagen, where, after the Germans glanced at his identity papers, he stepped ashore.

'Major Lund' was, in fact, Ole Lippmann, who had been sent from Copenhagen to London to be trained to work as England's chief organizer in the occupied capital. Although trained as a parachutist, at the last minute it appeared safer to bring him into Denmark on the Bornholm boat, a special route for top-priority Resistance people.

Lippmann had many jobs awaiting him in Denmark, and one of the most important was to keep an eye on what, in England, was now officially labelled 'Operation Shell House.' He was then the only man in Denmark who knew for certain that the raid was actually in the planning stage, although many other Resistance people hoped that this might be so.

In London, the planners worked feverishly. Having decided exactly how many aircraft would be needed, what bombs must be carried, how the planes would get into and out of Denmark, the only thing lacking was the order to attack.

Once more word was sent to Resistance people in Copenhagen that, if the attack were made, probably all the Danes in Shell House attic were doomed.

Ole Lippmann weighed this warning carefully and replied that, unfortunate as the risks were, the raid still ought to be made, for the hostages were being tortured, and if they were not killed in the bombing, they still had little chance of emerging from Shell House alive. One final distressing bit of information had helped make up Lippmann's mind.

The Gestapo office telephoned the Swedish Legation in Copenhagen that the minister must come to see the Germans at once, and Minister von Dardel was ushered in to see Dr. Hoffmann. The German announced: 'We're very angry with you Swedes. Very, very angry—and with good reason. We've learned that new Swedish weapons are being brought to the Danish Resistance from your country.'

'I'm afraid,' the minister replied, 'that I know nothing about it. Have you proof?'

Hoffmann ignored the question. 'Yours is still a neutral country, isn't it?' he asked.

'Yes, of course it is.'

'Well, then perhaps you'll be interested in these weapons. Have a look.' The Gestapo chief placed a new sub-machine gun on his desk. 'We've just captured six of these from the

Resistance. – quite new, and all identical. Go on—have a look at the maker's name.'

Minister von Dardel picked up the weapon. On it was the word '*Husquarna*'—Swedish beyond a doubt.

'I'll have to look into this matter. I must report it to Stockholm,' the minister said nervously.

'Do that,' Hoffmann replied. 'I'll be interested to hear what they have to say.

After the Swedish diplomat left Shell House, one of the first persons to hear about the captured Husquarna sub-machine guns was Ole Lippmann. Until that moment the Danish Resistance had wanted Shell House destroyed because it was a torture house, because it contained records that would destroy them. But now they knew it also held evidence that would condemn the kind help given to them by a neighbour. Lippmann sent an urgent radio message to England, and this time the reply seemed affirmative.

Sismore's squadron was then at a Second Tactical Air Force station at Rosières, in the Somme department of France, but they were ordered back to an aerodrome in Norfolk.

The attic of Shell House was full, not only of loyal Danes, for a quartet of informers were also housed there, trying to elicit information from the prisoners. The total number of Resistance men in the Shell House attic was twenty-five. On 1st March, after Lippmann's final message had been sent to England, Danish Army Captain Peter Ahnfeldt Mollerup, was taken. Mollerup knew—but never told the Germans or his fellow prisoners—of Lippmann's last message.

The day that this last prisoner was put in the attic, about seventy airmen gathered in the operations room at the Norfolk aerodrome to be addressed by Group-Captain Bob Bateson, who would lead the raid, and by Sismore and Truelsen. With them was a 'Wing-Commander Smith', a flier who wore no decorations, but only his pilot's wings. 'Smith' had flown

a Mosquito on the Aarhus raid, and he would be in the first
wave to hit Shell House. He was Air Vice-Marshal Embry.

In that briefing session were some of the finest R.A.F.
Mosquito pilots, men of 21, 464 and 487 Squadrons, Number
140 Wing of Two Group. The fighter pilots were also present.
Together they would attempt one of the most difficult air raids
of the war.

After Sismore had explained the navigational aspects of the
raid, Truelsen lectured on Shell House and what went on there.
The fliers were told about the men in the attic. Because of
them, Truelsen said, the bombs must hit the base of the building or the pavement in front of Shell House. And because of
the hostages, no incendiary bombs were being taken on the
raid. The idea would be to explode the records, not to burn
them. The two main staircases in Shell House were at either
corner in front, at the base of the U. These would certainly be
demolished, as would the one at the left rear of the building,
facing the lake, but Truelsen hoped that the stairs at the back
of the building, on the right side of the U, might be left undamaged. He was concerned about an escape route for the
men in the attic, not for the four hundred Nazis and Danish
traitors who worked in Shell House.

Should the fliers be shot down, Truelsen explained, they
were to contact Resistance people who would speed them to
Sweden.

Nothing seemed to have been left to chance, but the aircraft
would skim in over Copenhagen's rooftops at about three
hundred and fifty miles an hour—and Copenhagen's mass of
twisting streets and identical buildings even confuse pedestrians
unfamiliar with the city. To lead the raiders Truelsen had
volunteered to fly in the first aircraft, but because he was an
intelligence officer the British would not allow him to take
part in an action in which he might possibly be captured. As
Bateson's navigator, Sismore, never having visited Denmark, was
to find their way, and he had studied hard for the job.

The aircraft were to depart the morning after the briefing, and that evening the crews discussed the raid. If it worked, it would be monumental—and none of the airmen discussed what would happen if things went wrong. They knew they would be flying toward one of the most heavily defended of German positions.

The next morning bad weather again delayed the operation, but on the following morning the sky was clear and a strong wind blew across the Norfolk aerodrome. A lone Mosquito bomber taxied down the runway, rose, drew up its landing gear, and circled over the field. From the aircraft the pilot, 'Wing-Commander Smith', gave the order for the mission to begin. Two by two, first eighteen Mosquito bombers, then the faster twenty-eight P.51 Mustang fighters took off. Fifteen minutes later, as the Nazis and their Danish collaborators began their day's work in Shell House, Embry and his navigator, Squadron-Leader Peter Clapham, led the fliers across the North Sea toward Jutland.

19
The Shell House Raid

As soon as all the planes were in the air, Embry led them into a deep dive, and maintaining tight formation, they descended to about fifteen feet above the surf. Gale-force wind lashed at the North Sea, throwing up high salty spume that drenched the aircraft. Salt condensed on their windscreens—and there was no way to wipe it off.

To bomb Shell House before the Gestapo went to lunch, they must sneak all the way to Copenhagen, for if the German radar noticed them coming the attack would fail. Luftwaffe fighters would try to fend them off; or anti-aircraft batteries would slam them out of the sky. Only if they remained at fifteen feet, the sea blurring grey beneath them, would they not register bright pips on the German radar screens. Aerial counter-attacks against such low-flying planes would be virtually impossible.

The pilots and navigators in the Mosquitoes craned forward in their seats, for now the salt coated their windscreens solidly, and only a narrow slot across the screens' bottoms—no more than an inch and a half high—remained transparent. It was the blindest of blind flying, but they dared not climb.

And in the middle of chilly, windy Copenhagen, beneath a dun overcast sky, morning routine at Shell House was beginning normally. Several S.S. guards went to the attic to fetch Lyst Hansen, a loyal Danish police officer, who was to be taken that morning from Shell House to Vester Prison for immediate transfer to Frøslev Concentration Camp. Through the ventilation holes in their cell doors, Professor Brandt

Rehberg and several of the other prisoners saw Lyst Hansen led away.

When they reached the street, the policeman's S.S. guards looked around. 'Damn it!' one of them said. 'We've missed the car.' So the Dane was marched back up to his cell and locked away. He sprawled on the cot and opened a book.

On the fourth floor, in one of the Gestapo offices, a department head from the Danish Labour Ministry, a Mr. Høirup, was allowed to have a conversation with a Danish prisoner.

Out over the North Sea, the attackers now neared the south Jutland coast, and together they rose to a hundred and fifty feet. Jutland slipped quickly beneath them, then the grey water of the Little Belt, the green farms on the island of Funnen, the Great Belt's grey water, and finally green land once more. They had reached south Sealand.

Air Vice-Marshal Embry no longer gave the instructions, for, as planned, the aircraft were now to take their lead from Group-Captain Bob Bateson, whose Mosquito would be the first one in the first bomber wave to strike—if they got as far as the target.

In Copenhagen, a loud wail interrupted the morning. Air-raid sirens had gone off. The Germans had ordered them, but the city merely went on about its business, for everybody knew that this was just a routine morning test. Soon the sirens faded.

Sismore changed course to north-east until they were between Roskilde and Copenhagen, directly west of the capital. The eighteen Mosquito bombers now divided into three ranks of six each, and, over a lake, they formed a sort of three-spoked wheel in the air. After one lazy-looking rotation, the first six aircraft peeled off; and squinting through the small clear portion of his windscreen, Sismore could see the highway, Roskildevej, the road to Frederiksberg and then in to that cancerous building in the heart of crowded Copenhagen. Five more Mosquitoes were aligned on Sismore's right, close

together, moving in for a starboard attack. At one hundred and
fifty feet they flew onward at more than three hundred and
fifty miles an hour, the earth rushing in flashes beneath them.
Sismore watched carefully, giving Bateson the route, patiently
taking them toward Shell House.

Several S.S. guards had brought Poul Borking, a Danish
Army captain, down from the attic prison to the fifth floor,
to a Gestapo officer named Wiese who sat at a desk, his back
to the window. Through that window, over the German's
shoulder, Borking could see the broad lake, and beyond, the
silhouettes of Frederiksberg's blocks of flats. Both guards
remained in the room, their backs also to the window. Wiese
rose, went to the door, and departed, leaving Borking with
the S.S. guards.

At almost that same moment, several German soldiers
marched two Danish civilians, Taaning and Drescher, into an
office on the ground floor. Both were suspected of Resistance
activity. 'Now,' one of their guards ordered, 'let's have your
identity cards.'

At that moment there were thirty-two prisoners and four
Danish informers in the attic.

Sismore guided Bateson along a railway main line, then over
a vast goods yard. As they passed Frederiksberg, the navigator
saw the blur of a multi-coloured theatre marquee just below.
Ahead—the lake.

Captain Borking saw three flat specks emerge over
Frederiksberg's rooftops. The specks turned and grew, and
Borking could see what they were. His first impulse was to
yell a warning at his guards, for both now sat opposite him,
facing into the room. Thinking better of it, the captain moved
his hands slowly outwards, palms up, under the edge of the desk,
his eyes on the aircraft.

Upstairs, the prisoners in the attic now heard the oncoming
roar. Perhaps they could guess what it was, but what could
they do?

'Easy, now, easy—' Sismore said. And then, as the green and brown stripes he had been looking for appeared across the lake, he pointed and shouted excitedly, '*That building—there!*'

Now Bateson took over, eased his control forward, pointing his bomber's nose at the pavement in front of the building.

At that moment Borking tensed his muscles, rose, and tipped the desk forward—into the laps of the amazed Germans. Then, not hesitating, Borking ran out into the hall, hearing the two Nazis yell after him.

Bateson let his bombs go, felt the lightened aircraft lift. Then he tugged back the stick and wheeled away. The other five planes in that first wave had also skipped their high explosives into the bottom of Shell House. Those first two dozen bombs hit at about twenty minutes past eleven, and the whole building trembled. Mustang fighters flitted near by, spattering German anti-aircraft emplacements on the pink tile rooftops.

Captain Borking ran along the fifth-floor hall to the staircase at the right-hand side of the building. Excitedly his guards shouted after him, but Borking did not stop. He was at the third floor when, eleven seconds after they hit, the first bombs detonated.

As the first wave of Mosquitoes had let go their bombs, the Germans with Taaning and Drescher dropped the Danes' identity cards on a table, and, forgetting their prisoners, ran in panic toward the cellar. The two Danes headed for the outside doorway, but Taaning stopped and turned. 'Might need these!' he shouted, snatching up the identity cards. He and Drescher then fled from the building. The bombs had gone off, and already all the guards outside on the pavement lay dead, and the German car park across the way was a rubble heap. It was easy to keep on running. It was the only thing to do.

The prisoners in the attic, hearing the chatter of the Mustangs' machine guns and the shrill of the bombs, punched at their cell doors. Deep in Shell House, when the first missiles detonated, another shiver ran through the building, and the whole attic seemed to sway. In the tight cell block the plaster from the walls and ceiling flaked down, and dust clouds formed. Now the prisoners picked up their stools and began beating frantically at the plywood doors.

Out in front of Shell House some recently built air-raid shelters were pocked by shrapnel. Several bombs had gone into the German guardroom at the south-west corner of the building and exploded. Another that detonated in the cellar killed all the Danish Nazi translators. Two other bombs with long-delay fuzes were buried in the courtyard in the centre of the building.

Now—really too late—the air-raid sirens wailed, but they were engulfed by the tidal roar of the second bomber wave— but only five aircraft this time, for, over the Frederiksberg goods yard, the pilot of the second wave's leading Mosquito had been too low. His wing brushed a tall railway pylon. Out of control, he crashed into a building, and at the instant of impact his ton of bombs exploded and his petrol tanks were ablaze.

In the office of *Politiken*, in the Town Hall Square, reporter Carl Næsh-Hendriksen was pulling on an ambulance man's uniform. He would have to run out and give help—and, at the same time, try to get a story, not for his employers, the legal *Politiken*, but for the news service he fed, *Information*. First he would bicycle to the scene of the crashed bomber; Shell House, still under attack, would have to wait.

As the Labour Ministry official, Høirup, on his way from his interview with the Danish prisoner, reached the fourth floor, the first bombs had detonated. Høirup kept on down the stairs, but at the first floor he felt the building begin sinking from beneath him, and he was plunged into a dark room.

Captain Borking was only as far down as the third floor when the first bombs exploded. The staircase windows flew into slivers everywhere, and the officer nearly stumbled over a Wehrmacht soldier sitting dazedly against a wall. 'It's too late to run!' the German mumbled.

'Not yet!' Borking replied, and kept going. On the next landing sprawled another German soldier, blood spurting from his severed jugular vein. Borking kept on. By the time he reached the ground floor, he could feel intense heat from within the building.

Up in the attic the prisoners yelled. One bomb had sliced away the left wing of the prison block, and at least five cells were no longer there. Unable to force open his cell door with his fists, policeman Lyst Hansen hurled his stool at it. Almost too easily, he found he could get out. A middle-aged German in S.S. uniform, glassy-eyed, faced Lyst Hansen in the corridor. 'Give me the keys! Let me have the keys to the cells!' Lyst Hansen ordered.

The German seemed not to hear. Lyst Hansen's voice was partially drowned by the explosion of more bombs. Then the German muttered, 'Everything's going to end! Everything's going to end!'

Again Lyst Hansen shouted. 'The keys, man! The keys!' Slowly the German reached into his pocket, extracted something, and feebly held it out. A pair of scissors!

Lyst Hansen ran up to the guard, reached into his pockets, and found the large ring of keys.

One of the Mosquito bombers from the second wave now heeled eastward away from Shell House to drop a bomb on Dagmarhus, the other Nazi building, in the Town Hall Square. The plane had to skim over the German rooftop anti-aircraft emplacements, but the dazed guncrews had not yet uncovered their weapons, and, almost on the tail of the Mosquito, a Mustang dived to fire its six wing guns at the Germans on the roof.

One lone Luftwaffe fighter now approached Shell House, but its pilot, seeing the air so full of the wheeling British

aircraft—and apparently not wanting to risk being a hero—
turned and fled, foolishly triggering his guns to send a useless
spray of bullets over the centre of Copenhagen. Still no real
anti-aircraft fire had been flung at the British planes.

Captain Borking reached the bottom of the stairs and ran
out into the yard. The barbed-wire concertinas the Germans
had uncoiled in front of Shell House had been torn threadbare
by the first bomb, and Borking could run away from the
building easily.

The third wave of bombers now approached while, in the
attic, Lyst Hansen ran from cell to cell, unlocking doors and
flinging them open. He was surprised to find anyone alive in
the cell at the corner of the shattered west corridor, for a bomb
had taken away one wall and half the floor, and the cell was a
narrow shelf. Part of the roof was gone, and through the gap
the policeman could see the aeroplanes. He opened seventeen
cells. The last was that of Aage Schoch, a newspaper editor.
'Come now,' Lyst Hansen said calmly, 'it's time to go, Schoch.'

The men freed by the policeman ran toward the stairs at the
back of the building—the only one untouched. Maybe they
could still get out.

Høirup, of the Labour Ministry, made his way into a room
in the basement where he passed two German soldiers, one
already dead and the other badly wounded. Høirup did not
pause, and at the end of the hall he found a locked door, its
glass panels shattered. He got through it.

As Hans Heister stepped into the corridor, he saw two other
prisoners, Ove Kampmann and Professor Brant Rehberg. 'We
can't leave before they're all out,' one of them remarked calmly
to the other.

But, for the moment, the attic was quiet; everyone seemed to
have departed. Heister turned to retrieve a Bible from his cell;
back in the hallway he saw one more prisoner, dazed and
blinking, standing in a cell doorway. 'And now,' Kampmann
said, patiently leading the man, 'this way.'

As quickly as they could, the prisoners from the attic rushed down the stairs. Almost all of them reached the street, but three, including Poul Sørensen, a member of the Danish Parliament, and Paul Bruun, a businessman, were trapped in the cell block. Chased by the fire, they somehow managed to get through a window and began climbing down the outside of the building. However, they could only get down as far as the fourth floor. It was impossible to keep on going. On the lower floors of Shell House, despite the fact that no incendiary bombs had been used, flames churned through the destroyed Gestapo records, and the building was becoming an inferno. The three men clinging to the outside of Shell House looked down. On the pavement was a one-storey barracks. 'Maybe we can land on the roof—'

'It's risky, but we can't stay here.'

Hardly hesitating, all three men let go of their holds on the building.

Only one of the Danish informers in the attic had survived the attack to escape, and he was now fleeing with some of his compatriots he had betrayed.

Finally the Germans were shooting at the Allied aircraft— from the *Nürnberg*, tied in the harbour. Her guns brought down two Mosquitoes and one of the Mustangs.

As the third wave of aircraft roared toward Frederiksberg, the last of the Danes had fled the attic. Seeing the billowing smoke from the second-wave Mosquito that had crashed, noticing its flames jetting up through that smoke, the airmen in the last wave mistakenly thought that this was their target, and they loosed their bombs into buildings below them in Frederiksberg.

The bombing was now over, and all the planes that were not shot down had been able to get clear of the city. Several made light attacks on German camps north of Copenhagen before turning away toward Britain. Just over four minutes had passed since Sismore had first seen Shell House.

Lyst Hansen, Dr. Fog, and Aage Schoch had managed to get into the courtyard behind Shell House. Seeing a passage-way that led toward the street at the east side of the building, they ran through, under the only part of the Gestapo headquarters still relatively untouched.

In seconds, the whole of Shell House was a roaring fire, and much of the top of it had crumbled. Nothing was left of the cell block.

On the street, Lyst Hansen had seen no people, although from somewhere there was shooting. No time to waste looking around. He, Fog, and Schock had run until they reached the corner, and then hid behind the Technological Institute, adjacent to Shell House. A moment later a bomb had ripped through the roof. Their breath sucked out of them for a minute, the three men ran off in different directions, brushing dust from their clothes as they went.

When the bombing had started, several groups of Germans had been approaching Shell House, some in a big motor-car, and the rest on motor-cycles. These vehicles, empty, but with their engines still running, remained unattended outside the smoking building. Several of the escaped prisoners ran to them and drove off as more German soldiers, newly arrived, opened fire on them.

Næsh-Hendriksen arrived at Shell House to see Danes snatching up German weapons scattered all over the pavement in front of the burning building. One young man took a sub-machine gun under each arm and got away. No ammunition was strewn on the pavement, but from somewhere deep in the Shell House basement a magazine made a continuous loud popping as small-arms ammunition burned there.

Someone rushed up to help Poul Sørensen, whose legs had been broken in the leap. He had fallen on the barracks roof, slid to the pavement, and was still alive. Bruun was even more badly hurt. He had missed the one-storey barracks and landed in a barbed wire concertina on the pavement, and later one of his legs had to be amputated. The third man, taken with the other two to the German Military Hospital, died there after some hours. A fourth man, finding himself alone in the attic after the others had departed, could reach neither the stairs nor an outside window. Finally he had clambered out on to the roof, then jumped from there into the courtyard—and was killed by the fall.

Out over Samsø, between Sealand and Jutland, another of the Mosquito bombers was brought down by anti-aircraft fire. One of its crew was a Norwegian, a former Resistance man in his homeland, before he fled to Britain and trained with the R.A.F.

Captain Borking had rushed into an air-raid shelter, but seeing one of his German guards cowering in it, he ran off to another safe place. He was fairly far from Shell House when he heard the all-clear sound, and he climbed on a tram and rode away.

In Copenhagen, after some time, the two fires were put out. Shell House was gone, and the Gestapo records that might have trapped thousands of Danes were ruined. Two days after the raid, learning that five large safes were supposedly buried under the rubble, Holger Danske men took a lorry to the scene of the bombing. They were able to get the safes away to a moor, and to open them. Three were empty, but one contained a list of Danish Nazis that would be useful after the war. The fifth safe held only a German admiral's uniform. All the Husquarna machine-guns were lost to the Gestapo. Several hundred Nazis were killed, although many of the most important ones had been saved by a peculiar coincidence. Half an hour before the planes arrived, the top Gestapo men in Copenhagen gathered in a cemetery for the funeral of one of their colleagues who had died a few days before.

The Resistance managed to get as many of Shell House's loyal Danish survivors to Sweden as possible, and even the Danish informer who had escaped from the attic was taken across the Sound—by mistake. Of the prisoners in the attic, only six, including Admiral Hammerich and Captain Ahnfeldt Mollerup, the last man to be incarcerated, were dead. Twenty-seven had escaped.

But 'Operation Shell House', one of the most precarious low-level attacks of the war, although it achieved everything it set out to do, was an unhappy success. Four Mosquitoes and two Mustangs—ten airmen, altogether—had been lost. But there was a much worse catastrophe, for the Frederiksberg buildings that had been hit by the crashed Mosquito and then bombed by error was the Jeanne d'Arc School. Its casualties included some Catholic nuns and eighty-three children—just over a hundred people, altogether. Yet in crowded Copenhagen the necessity of the action was understood, and when Embry's airmen visited the city a week after the liberation, they were welcomed as heroes.

20
The Greatest Escape

AT the beginning of the occupation most Danish freighters were outside the country and began to sail under Allied merchant flags. The Danish shipyards the Germans compelled to build 'Hansa' class freighters found their production slowed by carefully scheduled sabotage. The Germans made the Danish Government pay for those 'Hansa' boats that were completed. Supposed to be working for the Germans, the boats were allowed by them to belong to a company created by the Danish Government. This, the Danes assured the Germans, would save the Nazi war machine the administrative nuisance that went with such ships. In fact, the Danes hoped that the ships would, under such a system, naturally revert to Danish ownership after the war. The officers of the Danish-French Steamship Company ran the 'Hansa' ships simply because their own vessels had all escaped internment at the beginning of the war, and the shipping company had no other work.

Usually the Danish 'Hansa' ships only appeared to be working for the Germans, for their operating company put the vessels on Denmark's various internal cargo services—to keep Denmark alive, the Germans were told. Had they studied Danish shipping reports more closely, the Germans might have learned that this was all a subterfuge.

By late March 1945 the first refugees from East Germany filtered into Denmark, where they were received coldly and lived in sordid squatters' camps. Was Copenhagen now to become a disembarkation port for milllions of East Germans? How could this unwanted immigration be stopped?

During those last months of the occupation, although ordinary Wehrmacht and German Navy personnel behaved correctly enough toward Danes, Gestapo and S.S. units became even more relentless in their pursuit of organized resistance, and they committed many so-called 'clearing' murders. In the end, the Danes feared, the Germans might show themselves capable of anything. Would the withdrawing forces spitefully try to wreck Danish shipping? Or almost as bad, would they attempt to make their retreat in Danish ships?

To block the port of Copenhagen, Resistance sabotage groups offered to blow up all the harbour bridges and operating machinery, but, eventually such damage would have had to be paid for by the Danes themselves. Very likely, any Allied bombardment of the port would have caused even costlier destruction. Also, whatever was done, the harbour would have to be usable again as soon as the Germans were gone.

A much more feasible plan had already been created late in 1944 by Ove Nielsen, the Danish permanent parliamentary secretary of the Ministry of Work, Shipping and Industry. In February and March of 1945, Nielsen's plan had been discussed and approved by Prince Axel, by the officers of the Danish–French Steamship Company, and by the heads of Copenhagen's Svitzer Salvage Company.

Svitzer's controlled most tug-boats in Denmark, and if these could be put out of operation, Denmark's major ports would suddenly become useless to the Germans. Could the tugs be taken to Sweden? Ove Nielsen believed they could, although he admitted that an incredible complex of deceptions would be needed—for no tug could ever sail without German authorization. And at no time in the past had German exit permits for so many tugs been given at one time. Nielsen realized that if only a few tugs fled to Sweden, the remainder would then have been put under such strict guard that they would never again have had the chance to escape. He also knew that any mass action might bring German reprisals against the seamen's families.

But Nielsen's plan would solve all the problems. It was a scheme as incredible as any naval action in Denmark's history— and the key to it was a mere 'Hansa' ship, the *Røsnæs.*

Before she was launched in 1944, *Røsnæs* had been sabotaged again and again, and she was only allowed by the Resistance to enter service after Captain Hahn-Petersen, head of the Danish-French Steamship Company, explained to underground leaders that the 3,000-ton vessel would haul brown coal, a fuel similar to peat, from Vejle, in Jutland, to Copenhagen for the city's gas-works to provide fuel for Danes, not Germans.

Early in April, the men who would supervise the carrying out of Nielsen's plan met to arrange final details. The captains of all the escaping vessels were to receive sealed orders, and none of the crews would have any warning of what was to happen. Captain Kiær, the managing director of Svitzer's, at first wanted the escape to be made on the night of Saturday, 7th April, but Captain Hahn-Petersen pointed out that this would be impossible because, according to her sailing schedule, *Røsnæs* would not have reached Copenhagen until the 4th, and she would not have discharged her cargo and be ready to leave in ballast until Sunday, the 8th. The officers finally agreed that Sunday would be the ideal day; most German port com-manders in Denmark would be away from their desks then. Also, if *Røsnæs* were sailing on Sunday, her crew could be given week-end leave until just before departure and this shore leave was vital to the plan.

When *Røsnæs* arrived on schedule from Jutland on 4th April, her decks covered with a thick patina of brown dust, her funnels belching sepia clouds—for she consumed the same bulky fuel as she carried—the Danish-French Steamship Company sent out word that the escape was ready to begin. The sealed orders were distributed.

Off the island of Møn, south of Sealand, a Danish freighter, the *Julius Madsen*, had struck a mine some weeks before, and Svitzer's ships had been at work on her until bad weather made all their attempts to salvage the vessel futile. The weather had not improved, but Svitzer's asked German port authorities in Copenhagen to let tugs return to Møn to resume operations, and a tug, *Garm*, with two divers aboard, was allowed to go there the day after the *Røsnæs* docked. *Garm* arrived at the sunken ship on 6th April, and the same day another tug, *Svana*, asked to be allowed to help with the *Julius Madsen*. *Svana* was given clearance. *The first two boats were now ready to escape.*

The same day, the Svitzer tug *Brage* towed a lighter out of Copenhagen, and was due back in the capital, the Germans were told, three days later. *A third boat was now ready.*

Two more Svitzer vessels, *Sigyn*, which was in Copenhagen, and *Vulcan*, in Naksov, a port at the southern end of the Great Belt, each applied for permission to sail down to Gedser to tow a disabled state ferry to Copenhagen for repairs. Since the Gedser ferry usually sailed to Warnemünde, in Germany, and was vital to the Germans, this permission was granted at once.

Vulcan set out on 5th April, and *Sigyn* on the 6th—but neither went to Gedser. Instead, just before lunch on the 7th, they joined the other two salvage boats at the *Julius Madsen*. A German patrol boat, on a routine sweep off Møn that afternoon, passed near enough to notice that all four salvage boats were apparently carrying out diving operations, and the Germans did not stop to watch or to report seeing the boats. These four tugs were now in position to run toward Trelleborg, in southern Sweden. *Five boats were ready.*

In Kalundborg, a large port in north-west Sealand, were two of Svitzer's heavy tugs that did salvage and towing in the Great Belt. The company told the Germans about negotiations to pull up and tow a sunken Danish freighter, the *Otto Petersen*, out of Oslofjord, and the Germans readily gave permission for this operation—which would no doubt have surprised the

Otto Petersen's captain, for although his ship was in the Norwegian inlet, she was moored, and not sunk there.

Two tugs, *Freja* and *Ægir*, left Kalundborg for Norway, taking in tow two large salvage pontoons, *Odin* and *Thor.* Originally supposed to sail on the 7th, the captains of the tugs heard that rumours that they would run to Sweden were circulating on the Kalundborg docks, so both officers decided to move their ships out into Kalundborgfjord at once, and to spend the night of the 6th moored there. The following morning, at seven o'clock, they set out to sea, but instead of following the route eastward along the Jutland coast and then north to Norway, they headed directly north and into the Kattegat. But because they had departed nearly twelve hours ahead of the time set in their orders, the two vessels first made for a sunken Norwegian freighter, the *Utviken*, and then lay at anchor near her. *Seven tugs were now ready to escape.*

Another tug, the *Urd*, left Kalundborg.the same day at lunchtime to get a steamer, the *Desdemona*, which was sunk off Gilleleje, on the north Sealand coast. *Now eight tugs were ready.*

By then it was almost time for *Røsnæs* to begin her part in the operation—but her plans were more involved. As part of these plans, on the morning of 8th April, a young Resistance man went to the Danish-French Steamship Company's office and asked to be signed as a crew member on the *Røsnæs*. Various shipping regulations, he was told, made this quite impossible.

'But I must be aboard her,' he insisted. 'It's vital.'

'Don't worry,' Mr. Lage, the head clerk in the Danish-French office said. 'Everything will be taken care of. Just wait and see.'

That same afternoon, another Resistance man visited the shipping office with a neatly wrapped paper parcel which he left with Mr. Nyholin, confidential clerk in the office.

Early the following morning, 9th April, four Resistance men used forged passes to get into Copenhagen's Free Harbour to

the pier of a Danish weapons factory. The Germans maintained a strong guard at this quay, but since the Danes were
unarmed and their papers seemed to be in order, they were not
bothered. When *Røsnæs* arrived in the Free Harbour, she had
already cleared the German customs control that covered the
southern part of the Sound, and had undergone the routine
German search. Since the vessel was not to sail until noon,
her crew left on their usual Sunday shore leave, and the captain
came off the ship to lead the four Resistance men aboard to an
anchor chain locker. 'Make yourselves comfortable here,' he
told them.

When the crew of the freighter returned, the Germans
merely checked the ship's clearance papers, and seeing that a
customs and military check had already been made, did not
bother to come aboard. This, Ove Nielsen had supposed, was
exactly what would happen.

At ten o'clock in the morning the two largest, most modern
tugs in Copenhagen, Svitzer's *Gorm* and *Ymer*, left their
moorings for Odense, northward by way of Elsinore, for a
routine towing task. *Ten tugs were now clear.*

Just before *Røsnæs* departed at lunchtime, Mr. Nyholm took
the paper parcel to Captain Hartz-Rasmussen aboard the
freighter. It was last-minute cargo for Jutland, the clerk
explained with a wink. As he directed his ship out of the Free
Harbour, Captain Hartz-Rasmussen was worried. A slight
north-west breeze had wafted away all the mist from the
Sound—and he had been promised at least a little fog. Oh well,
it could not be helped.

Early in the afternoon Svitzer's office sent a telegram to
Frederikshavn, in North Jutland, to the tugs *Mjølner* and *Odin*,
instructing them to get permission to run over to Læsø Island,
half-way between Jutland and Sweden, to rescue a stranded
schooner. With their telegram as authority, the two tugs'
captains went to the German port office for clearance, but the
Germans would not let them go. Worried, the Danes asked

why. The Germans said they expected a troop transport to arrive soon, and the tugs would be needed to bring her in. These two boats would be unable to escape.

On the Danish shore of the Sound the only people who watched *Røsnæs* through glasses that afternoon were Resistance men. Instead of following the western channel along the Danish coast, *Røsnæs* veered eastward toward the island of Hven, half-way between Denmark and Sweden. The waters around the island were Swedish—shallow, but with a soft, sandy bottom.

Aboard *Røsnæs*, Captain Hartz-Rasmussen watched tensely from his bridge. His orders had been to head for the north-east side of Hven, but now he saw a German patrol boat just ahead. Thinking quickly, the captain told his quartermaster to turn hard to starboard, and moments later the two men heard a loudly echoing rasp as *Røsnæs* lurched and ran aground in the smooth sand near Hven—just as Ove Nielsen had planned. A few minutes later, the four Resistance men mounted Captain Hartz-Rasmussen's bridge. 'You have a parcel for us, captain?'

'Just a minute,' the officer grinned, getting the package from his cabin.

'Now, sir, will you please give us our guns so we can hold you up and take command of the ship?' the Resistance men asked politely.

The captain helped the men unwrap and load their weapons. 'But, for God's sake, be careful with these!' he said. 'They look like antiques!'

'Don't worry, captain. But surely you don't want us to have decent weapons confiscated in Sweden?'

At two-thirty that afternoon, in the Danish–French Steamship Company's offices in Copenhagen, Mr. Nyholm received a cable that had been composed, in part, in his office the day before. 'RØSNÆS AGROUND HVEN SOUTH SHOAL. STANDING HARD. QUICK AND HEAVY ASSISTANCE NEEDED. TIDE RUNNING OUT. HARTZ.'

Nyholm telephoned Svitzer's where a similar distress signal from *Røsnæs* had already been received. Svitzer's had already contacted the marine insurance offices that covered the 'Hansa' freighter, and now were going through the usual formalities to get assistance to the stranded ship. A signal explaining this was sent to Captain Hartz-Rasmussen who, still on his bridge, was now technically a prisoner of the Resistance. 'For heaven's sake be careful with those weapons,' the captain cautioned.

'Don't worry,' the Resistance men laughed. 'If we pulled the triggers on these old things, we'd probably blow our own heads off!'

When the German harbour master's clerk in Copenhagen was shown the message from *Røsnæs*, he permitted the Svitzer tug, *Pluto*, to go out to the stranded ship. *Pluto* left at three o'clock in the afternoon, and at six the lighter's captain was allowed to tow a barge, the *Tyr*, out to help unload the *Røsnæs*—although the lighter's captain was perfectly aware that the freighter's cargo holds would be empty. *Twelve vessels were now ready to escape.*

By then Copenhagen's harbour was without tugs, and Svitzer's office asked the Germans for permission to order the *Mars* and *Alert*, both salvage tugs, down from Elsinore to the *Rosnæs* because the freighter was aground in such dangerously shallow water. The Germans said this would be all right, and on their way, according to Ove Nielsen's plan, the two tugs encountered *Gorm* and *Ymer*, on their way to Odense. The captain of the *Mars* signalled the other two ships to come about and head down to assist with the emergency work off Hven Island. *Fourteen vessels were now ready to escape.*

Toward dusk, fine mist began settling over the water, and the *Røsnæs* was no longer visible from the Danish shore of the Sound—which was just as well, because the Germans were unable to see that the freighter now had five tugs and a lighter clustered around her—enough vessels to get her free in a few minutes.

The two pontoon-towing ships, at anchor for some hours at the Norwegian freighter in the Kattegat, now cast off for Anholt Island, planning to keep on course until late at night, then to turn starboard to race into the Swedish port of Halmstad.

Would the Germans grow curious and cross over into Swedish waters to visit the *Røsnæs*—and order the boats with her to return to their Danish ports? To prevent such a move, the Swedes had agreed to send out a motor torpedo boat which reached the stranded freighter at quarter to seven in the evening, and then began slowly circling in the area.

At eight-thirty Svitzer's office manager again telephoned the German port authorities in Copenhagen. He was worried, the salvage company official said, because he had had no word from *Røsnæs* for some hours. 'Her wireless must be out of order,' he explained. 'Can we send out a tug to see what's happening?'

The Germans, suspecting nothing, gave their consent for another tug, *Activ*, to be dispatched for Hven at nine o'clock. *Now fifteen boats were in a position to get away.*

When the *Activ* reached the sands off Hven, she found considerable confusion. Fortunately, Captain Kiær, the head of the Svitzer Company, had arrived earlier in one of his tugs and the captains of all the vessels accepted his orders to stand by. Several other salvage vessels at smaller ports along the Danish side of the Sound had heard the first distress signals put out by the *Røsnæs*, and these boats had come out on their own initiative to help tow the freighter off the sand bank. This had not been part of Ove Nielsen's scheme, but it was all to the good of the operation, for the captains on these boats accepted Captain Kiær's orders without question. *By now, nineteen Danish vessels were ready to escape.*

Ove Nielsen's plan said there would be no actual signal for the final escapes, but each of the vessels would act on its own orders, independently of the others. Thus, the day before the *Røsnæs* departed from Copenhagen, the *Urd* had already left the sunken *Desdemona* near Gilleleje, and was by now on her way to Höganäs in Sweden, where she arrived at one o'clock on the morning of 9th April.

Also on the 8th, the four salvage vessels with the *Julius Madsen* began casting off. The first left the sunken ship at nine-thirty in the evening, and the others followed at half-hourly intervals. The last one arrived at three-thirty on the morning of the 9th in the roads off Trelleborg Harbour in Sweden, and all four vessels were guarded through the night by Swedish naval ships which escorted them into the harbour at dawn.

The two tugs with pontoons—supposedly going to Oslo-fjord—turned toward Sweden from Anholt Island in the Kattegat, and docked in Halmstad at four in the morning. And *Brage*, the tug that had towed a lighter out from Copenhagen on the 6th, also arrived in Sweden on schedule.

A little later in the morning, *Røsnæs*, like a worried hen surrounded by her clucking chicks, was towed easily off the sand, and at quarter to seven in the morning, she and the tugs and lighters pulled into Landskrona, in Sweden, to be interned. Nielsen's operation had been completed. *Nineteen vessels were sneaked safely out of Denmark.*

When the Svitzer offices in Copenhagen opened, only two staff members were there, for all the other employees had departed as stowaways on the tugs. Later, when German port authorities stormed into the salvage company's office with a list of the escaped vessels, the two men pretended to be dumb-founded. Then one said lamely, 'But the tugs *Dan* and *Thor* are still in Denmark.' Neither Dane explained that these vessels had been left behind because they were too small to be of much use to the Germans.

From Sweden the Germans received a report that *Røsnæs* had been overpowered by the Resistance, and believing this probably also happened to the other vessels, the Nazis ordered no reprisals against the seamen's families. Later in the day the

Germans went to the offices of the Danish-French Steamship Company but found that all the heads of the organization were away from their desks. These men moved underground and did not reappear until the liberation.

Next the German Naval Command in Denmark sent out an immediate order for the confiscation of the two tugs that had not been able to get clearance to leave Frederikshavn. At first the Germans tried to run these vessels themselves, but this proved so inefficient that Danes were put back on the boats.

The Germans kept the port of Copenhagen in operation— but things went slowly. Although many ships were able to come and go without tugs, the larger vessels dared not move, and it was quite impossible for the Germans to steal Danish ships either for the movement of refugees or for their final retreat.

When she was run aground, the *Røsnæs* was more badly damaged than the Danes had expected, but she had enough salvage ships on hand to get her ready in time to be the first vessel to return to Denmark after the liberation, with a full load of troops of the Danish Brigade.

21
The Sound

ARLY in 1945, a Danish Resistance intelligence agent returning from Stockholm to Copenhagen was concerned when the small boat taking him across the Sound was slowed by fog. Soon the outline of the Danish coast was obscured by mist. 'Have you got a compass?' the agent asked his fisherman pilot.

'Yes, of course. Don't worry.'

The fog became cotton wool. 'Where are we going to land in Copenhagen?'

'You'll know soon enough. Don't worry.'

Peering ahead is they drifted, the agent suddenly distinguished something ashore—a fortress, but he did not know which one. 'Are you *sure* you know where we are?'

'Well,' the fisherman apologized, 'not exactly.'

'But you said this boat had a compass!'

'And so she has—but it doesn't work.'

Yet the agent landed safely and was working in Copenhagen in the morning as planned. He need not have worried, for in situations far worse, Denmark's illegal transport still got through. On the Sound, five regular routes carried more than 18,000 passengers—some of them many times. This fleet, along with the Gothenburg-Jutland boats, the Bornholm steamers, and the fishing vessel from Blyth, moved a greater tonnage of resistance materials into Denmark than were air dropped there—and little of the boats' cargo was intercepted.

No other occupied country had such strong links with the free world outside. Neither trigger-happy sentries ashore nor coastal patrol vessels kept the Danes from crossing the Sound. A complex system of permanent minefields made their illegal crossings precarious, and the Allies worsened things—for the Danes as well as the Germans—by dropping magnetic mines that drifted with the tides. Yet during the last years of the occupation, both the mail and passenger services between Denmark and Sweden were faster on the illegal boats than on normal peacetime carriers.

Co-ordinated in Stockholm, none of the five routes knew of the movements of the others, for this would have been bad security. When, by accident, the crews on one route crossed the path of a vessel from another, both boats fled, each afraid the other might be German.

Although they operated under the worst of conditions, not all of the transport men were seamen. Leif B. Hendil, for example, was a seasick-prone Copenhagen journalist. After helping many friends escape to Sweden, Hendil had to quit Denmark himself in the early autumn of 1943. Ebbe Munck gave him 80,000 Swedish kroner which had been collected by Swedish Jews, and the journalist bought a boat. By the war's end, Hendil's Malmø-based fleet—by then eleven vessels— had carried more than 2,000 passengers, including more than forty Allied airmen and another forty Allied civilians on the run, without once losing a passenger. Like the other boats, their freight included Bibles and guns, school books and school-children, money and mail, and anything else the Resistance wanted smuggled across the Sound. And on his many clandestine crossings, Hendil never disgraced himself by being seasick.

Max Weiss, a Copenhagen police official, set up another route from Sweden, and Danish naval officers, forced underground in 1943, used their knowledge of the Sound to run their own shipping service and to help keep the other boats going. Arne Sejr's students sometimes confounded the Germans by landing their groups' boats in tiny Hellerup Harbour, almost in the centre of Copenhagen. Although the yacht basin is marked quite clearly on the city's port charts, the Germans never discovered it, and it remained unobserved throughout the war!

Many of the boats drew up at a rubbish dump near an old Danish fortress on the island of Amager. Three hundred Germans were quartered in the fort, and the Resistance quay was within a few yards of its sentry post. Yet by moving cautiously and obeying torch signals given by a loyal Dane who guarded the dump, every night dozens of people boarded or disembarked from boats there.

During the boats' first busy period, when the Jews were being sped to Sweden, passengers had to embark in the daytime in Copenhagen's busiest harbours. The Germans hired civilian informers to watch the boats, but the Danes contrived to fool them. When the boats were docked, Danes streamed steadily on and off them, so that no matter how carefully the spies watched, they could never keep an accurate count of how many people remained aboard. Secret passenger compartments in many of the larger trawlers and coasters took hours for the Germans to find, so they began using search dogs. Leif Hendil found a way to thwart the animals.

Seeing dogs led aboard their boats, the captains would pretend to blow their noses, then shake out their handkerchiefs. After that, the dogs never located their quarry, for the handkerchiefs held a special grey powder. Concocted by a Danish chemist in Malmø, it contained a mixture of dried human blood and cocaine, and it deadened the dogs' sense of smell.

Hendil also solved the greatest of problems—that of getting money to keep the boats going. In Sweden he canvassed Danish Jews who had been brought to safety. Few of them had taken much money with them, but all gave promissory notes, and Ebbe Munck found a contact in the Danish Treasury who managed to have the money advanced through secret government sources in Copenhagen. It was all repaid after the war, and because of it, Denmark's boats never had to rely on a single penny of Allied funds.

Without Swedish help, the boats could not have sailed. The neutral authorities arranged special harbours where the Danes could work unobserved by German agents. The Danish crews were allowed to move freely in Sweden, and even bonded warehouses were thrown open to them so that, on cold nights, the passengers could fight the chill with duty-free brandy. During the last days of the war the boats from Sweden landed in Denmark, although at first all passengers were transhipped in mid-water. Yet from the beginning the boats usually flew Swedish flags, and the authorities pretended not to notice. Many of the Danish seamen escaped the German patrols by pretending to be Swedes.

Most of the illegal transports on the Sound were un-glamorous diesel fishing vessels, but speedboats and whatever other ships were available were also used. Servicing the boats was seldom a critical problem, for Swedish engineering firms provided spare parts, and many Danish mechanics had entered Resistance work. One of the engineers for the faster boats was an aircraft mechanic whose arrival in Sweden was most spectacular.

Per Juhl serviced German aircraft at Kastrup Aerodrome. One day when he and another Dane were at work in a Heinkel twin-engined bomber, Juhl asked, 'Do you know how to fly one of these things?'

'No,' his friend replied.

'Nor do I. Let's try.'

'You're crazy!' the other mechanic said, running from the aircraft.

Minutes later Juhl taxied down the Kastrup runway—for his maiden flight. The Germans fired at him, but he was able to take off. He had thought of going to England, but he noticed his fuel gauges almost registered empty, so he pointed the Heinkel east toward Sweden.

When Swedish fighters came out to meet him, Juhl remembered that he had no idea how to land an aeroplane, and he left the controls. Nervously climbing as far back into the tail as he could get, he began doing the only other thing he could think of. He prayed.

The only part of the Heinkel not completely demolished in the crash was the tail section, and Juhl climbed out unhurt.

But if Juhl's adventure was spectacular, it was no more so than the things that began to happen on the Sound when the time came for the Resistance boats to enter into active warfare against the Germans.

In the autumn of 1943, during the evacuation of the Jews, the Danish harbour pilots had begun Resistance work. Their credentials allowed them to go anywhere in the port, and they knew how to navigate through the minefields in relative safety. Some of them, like Captain Erik Larsen, the chairman of the Danish Pilots' Association, operated Resistance transports at night while piloting German ships during the day.

Late in 1944 the twenty-two Copenhagen harbour pilots told the Germans that they would no longer work at night; they were sick and tired of being sniped at by nervous German patrols. The Germans were furious. 'Tell your pilots,' a Gestapo officer ordered Captain Larsen, 'that if they stop night work, we'll take ten of them out and shoot them.'

The pilots ignored the German threat, but the Gestapo dared take no reprisals. The pilots were too vital to port operation.

In the beginning of January 1945 the pilots said they wanted to stop all work for the Germans, but when Larsen passed this on to Resistance leaders, they told him that his men must keep at their posts until London ordered their flight to Sweden. 'But we could take our boats over now,' Larsen protested. 'They would be more useful in Sweden.'

'No, Captain, we must let London decide.'

The Copenhagen port commander was then a German

merchant navy officer who knew that ambulances took wounded Resistance people through his territory to the illegal boats, that there was contact between the Danish and Norwegian Resistance organizations by way of boats that docked in Copenhagen, and that his German port guards were lured away by free drinks when Resistance activity was beginning in the port. He notified the Gestapo of none of these things. And if the pilots disappeared, Resistance leaders said, the Germans might decide to replace this kindly officer with someone more severe.

German shipping traffic in Copenhagen was increasing, and again and again the pilots asked the Resistance to be allowed to stop helping this. But the Resistance insisted the pilots stay at work.

In March, without explanation, the Gestapo took over Copenhagen harbour. The lenient port officer was sent home to Germany, and all the harbour area patrols were strengthened. Again the pilots asked if they could leave.

An explanation of the new state of things went to England, and London decided the pilots could leave. But now they were stuck, for all of their identity papers had just been called in by the Gestapo, and the pilots could not leave Copenhagen harbour without them—not in their boats, anyway.

Meanwhile, aggressive actions were beginning in the Copenhagen port. Danish naval cadets sank a disused freighter in the mouth of Langebro, a part of the harbour, sealing in a special German minesweeper equipped to cope with sonic mines. Then the tugs escaped to Sweden.

On a Thursday in mid-April Larsen went to the Gestapo. 'Can we have our identity papers back? My men can't work without them.'

Suspicious that something was about to happen, the Germans refused to give back the papers, and no ships entered or left the harbour. On Friday, Larsen again approached the Germans and again the papers were withheld. But on Saturday, noticing that all the pilots were still apparently in Copenhagen, the Gestapo decided to return the credentials. The pile-up of German ships in the Sound was getting uncomfortable.

That night Larsen arranged to have three Copenhagen pilot boats, one from Elsinore, and three in other ports, readied for sailing. He telephoned the Germans that the boats were going out to guide a convoy into port, and he and some other Copenhagen pilots took their three boats out past Langelinie. It was no easy job, for an over-eager saboteur had smashed the engine of Larsen's vessel. But eventually the ship was made to run, and the pilots slipped past the cruiser *Nürnberg*, past the German patrol ships in the harbour mouth, and over to Malmø. Almost all of the other Danish pilots who did not take their boats to Sweden went underground in Denmark. Copenhagen now had no one who could manoeuvre ships through the minefields. Hundreds of German ships would be unable to get in or out.

The Gestapo sent for German pilots, but in unfamiliar waters they were slow; and approached by the Resistance, these Germans, realizing the war was lost, agreed to continue to move ships with hyper-cautious slowness. After all, why hurry, and risk blowing themselves up in the minefields?

In Malmø, Captain Larsen reported to Danish naval officers who assigned him to the Malmø speedboat fleet. By then there were five speedboats, mainly American Chris-Craft, capable of between twenty-eight and forty knots. Most of their seats had been removed to make the boats more spacious, and rubber extensions had been fitted to their exhausts, so that near shore these could be held under water, making the boats almost noiseless. Painted dull grey, they attracted little attention. At high speeds they could charge straight through the minefields, and if they set off any mines they would be safely out of the way before the charges detonated. Rough seas were their only problem, for although they could skim over the waves easily enough, the turbulence made their compass cards spin like roulette wheels, and on the best nights for operations visual navigation was usually impossible.

Yet running guns, carrying courier messages, and transporting Resistance men who had to cross the Sound quickly, Larsen's speedboats continually outwitted the Germans. Always armed with Sten guns, pistols, and grenades, the Danes even penetrated the innermost parts of Copenhagen harbour. They once went there to reconnoitre the position of a small German warship. Moving in the shadows, they drew right alongside the vessel, but they had not expected to be so lucky, and they had no mines they could place. The following night, when they returned with the mines, the Germans had set up spotlights around the ship, and closing with her was then impossible.

Another evening, Malmø received a message that a Resistance boat had hit a shoal and was taking in water near the south Sealand coast. She was full of guns, and if she did not move before daylight the Germans would find her. Larsen sped across the Sound to the disabled boat. While some of his men tried to pump out her water, the others transhipped the cargo to make towing away the damaged craft easier. A German patrol boat was somewhere in the area, the Danes knew, but they worked silently. Suddenly there was a flash and a loud rattling noise. One of the Resistance men had caught the trigger of a loaded Sten gun against something and discharged an entire magazine. Almost all of the bullets tore through the man's thigh.

Larsen heard shouts from far off; and a searchlight beam raked toward them. He had already moved the speedboat so that it obscured the disabled boat from view. 'Get down quickly!' he hissed.

Maybe the Germans would not come to investigate if they saw only one boat in their light. If the men remained below the gunwales, maybe the Germans would think the shooting had come from the nearby Danish shore.

The searchlights swept back and forth, and the men, crouching nervously, put a tourniquet on the leg of their wounded companion. Luckily there were spirits aboard the speedboat, and Larsen forced the wounded man to down an entire bottle.

For anxious minutes the searchlight fanned near them, but when it faded, the Danes heard the German patrol boat start her engines. Tensely the Resistance men waited, but the sound of the other boat died away. The Germans apparently had decided nothing was wrong. From the island of Hven, on the Swedish side of the Sound, Larsen telephoned Malmø to have an ambulance await his boat in Sweden.

On another evening, Danes in Malmø were told that the passenger liner coming from Bornholm to Copenhagen had aboard several uniformed Danes who worked for the Germans. The war was nearly over, and the Resistance were afraid that these traitors would merge into the Danish civilian population. Could the speedboats do something about this?

Two of the craft were rushed out in the direction of Bornholm, and when the liner came into sight, one speedboat pulled up on either side, then slowed down to nestle against the moving ship. Several men from each of the small boats silently boarded the liner. Unobserved on her deck, the well-armed Resistance men covered all of the companionways to the passengers' cabins. Erik Larsen then went on to the bridge to see the captain, an old friend. When Larsen explained why the liner must be interned in Malmø, her captain agreed to cooperate. 'But, for God's sake, Larsen, poke a gun in my back and make me do it! The war isn't over yet!'

The Swedes willingly interned the boat and imprisoned not only the Danish traitors but also a Gestapo officer who was aboard. But the neutral authorities refused to do everything the Resistance men wanted. 'You'll have to give those Nazis back their uniforms,' they insisted. 'We refuse to let them come ashore naked!'

Larsen's most complex speedboat task had been first

requested when he was still at his post in Copenhagen. 'Sorry,'
he had replied, 'but it can't be done from this side of the Sound.'
The Resistance wanted him to obscure all the buoys from the
island of Møn, south of Sealand, to a point opposite Malmø,
cutting off the best mine-swept channel in the last twenty miles
of water from the Baltic to Copenhagen. Larsen agreed to do
the job from Malmø, but it would be difficult.

Damaging the lights on the buoys would not be enough; the
big iron floats would have to be sunk, and because the Danes
knew nothing about their construction, placing of the
explosives would be a matter of chance. Timing of the work
would have to be planned carefully so that no Resistance transport would be accidentally harmed. The speedboat would
sometimes have to idle through the minefields, and maybe there
would not be a chance to run from accidental explosions.
Worse, they were almost certain to encounter German patrols.
There was no way to avoid this, for one German ship always
patrolled at the Møn end of the channel.

At six o'clock one mid-April evening, Larsen set out in a
Chris-Craft piloted by Erik Stærmose, a Danish naval officer,
and with another Dane named Møller. They raced directly
toward Møn, then cautiously criss-crossed the waters there,
looking for the channel markers. But in the thin fog they
could not find the buoys or take bearings from the Danish
coast. They were wasting precious hours; they had to be
finished by dawn.

Finally Larsen gave the order to head north; they would
attack the markers from the other end of the channel. At least
they had not yet met any Germans.

The northern markers were easier to see, and all three Danes
kept busy. Møller held Larsen's legs so that the pilot could
fasten the limpets about three feet below the water's surface.
Using two-hour time pencils they had had to waterproof
themselves, they hoped their charges would detonate.

'See any Germans yet?' Larsen asked.

'No, not yet.

From buoy to buoy they crept. The night was icy and some of the lights burned dim and were hard to find. So far, no Germans.

Daylight began to break before four o'clock, and they had not yet finished. Only fishing boats passed them.

Looking for one of the last buoys, they saw a boat—and she was moored not two hundred yards from the buoy. 'Hell!' said Stærmose. 'She's a German motor torpedo boat!'

'Pretend to polish the light when we get to the buoy,' Larsen ordered. Through glasses he studied the other vessel. One man was on deck watching them. If the Germans came close, they could blow the speedboat out of the water, or nearly as bad, search her and find the limpets.

All three Danes now worked over the buoy, pretending to service it. Larsen raised his glasses again and watched the German. 'He's going below!' Larsen said. 'Quick! Stick on the limpet!'

Larsen then saw the German come on deck and begin to raise something. Squinting, the Dane saw it was a pair of glasses. When the German waved, Larsen, Stærmose, and Møller waved back.

Just as Stærmose started their engine, a loud booming came over the water. 'Damn!' said Larsen. 'Our first mine's gone off! Back to Malmø! Hurry!'

Looking over his shoulder, Larsen saw the German patrol craft shiver as her engines started. If she chased them she would probably use her guns.

Stærmose raced the engine full throttle, and the Chris-Craft shot high over the waves toward Malmø. The German boat, instead of following them, turned and ran toward the northern end of the minefield to investigate the explosion.

The Germans were unable to reach any of the limpets in time, and although some of the buoys did not sink entirely below the surface, the channel was effectively obscured.

In Malmø plans were made for speedboats to land small boarding parties on the fortresses at the mouth of Copenhagen harbour to kill the German troops there. All the lighthouses in south Sealand were to be raided by Danes who would kill the German guards and steal vital parts of the lights that could be restored when peace came. Another speedboat was to attack the channel buoys between Copenhagen and Elsinore.

Like many of the most ambitious Resistance plans, these operations were not carried out because the war ended too soon. Nevertheless, more than four hundred and fifty German ships were unable to get out of Danish harbours before the liberation. During those last days of Denmark's war, Resistance seamen had gained full supremacy of the waters around the country.

22

A Good Night's Sleep

TOWARD the end of the occupation, Jens Lillelund was in Jutland, where he trained saboteurs and organized attacks against German troop trains. Although the Jutland Resistance radio kept receiving orders for his return to Sweden, Lillelund pretended not to hear. He was too busy. Finally, early in 1945, he went to Stockholm; and he was flown at once by Mosquito bomber to London. 'Why,' Lillelund asked S.O.E., 'did you send for me?'

'We're going to train you as a saboteur, and then parachute you into Denmark to organize sabotage actions.'

Lillelund stared incredulously. 'But I *was* in Denmark, and I *was* organizing sabotage actions!'

The S.O.E. officers then explained that British troops might have to fight their way into Denmark. Lieutenant Lillelund—like many Danish Resistance leaders sent to Britain, he was commissioned in the Buffs—was to organize special co-operative action. Lillelund trained and waited.

In Denmark red, white, and blue arm-bands were being prepared for issue to the underground fighters who would emerge on a signal from the West. Now no sabotage action was staged unless the cost of repairing its damage was offset by military necessity. Informers and collaborators were, when possible, abducted to Sweden to be interned. Others were kept under close watch. Resistance groups systematically looted German records, for everything the occupying force had done must be catalogued. The same Danish thoroughness that had controlled the Resistance now groped for the post-war reins.

In February 1945 Ebbe Munck asked Leif Hendil for an unusual favour. Arranging details of the operation on the Copenhagen side of the Sound, Hendil found, was not so difficult, but when he told Richard Hansen, the Danish-born chief of police in Malmø, what was to be done, Hansen protested, 'Not through my port! Suppose the Germans found out?'

'They won't,' Hendil assured him.

What Hendil was to do was to try to smuggle an Englishman into Copenhagen—and out again. Hansen objected because this Englishman, as far as Hendil knew, spoke no Danish. How could he move about in Copenhagen undetected? What if he were caught and said he had come over from Malmø?

'Suppose,' Hendil suggested, 'I make this Englishman into a Dane?'

'I don't think you can do it,' Hansen replied, 'but there's no harm in trying.'

On the morning of 4th March, Frank Pinnock arrived in Malmø and reported to Hendil. The journalist later described the tall, thin, slightly balding, forty-two-year-old temporary civil servant as 'the best type of international Englishman'.

'Ebbe Munck told me to put myself completely in your hands, Mr. Hendil. He said you'd arrange everything.'

'Well, we've a lot to do,' Hendil answered. He led Pinnock into a bedroom. 'Now, sir, would you please be so kind as to get undressed?'

Pinnock stared quizzically.

Hendil smiled. 'This has to do with making you into a Dane.'

All the labels in Pinnock's English clothing were replaced by Danish ones. His shoes, unmistakably British, were taken from him, and he was lent a pair of Hendil's. Pinnock's pockets were emptied, and he was given Danish stamps, coins, a tram ticket, and even membership cards for various clubs in Copenhagen. Identity photographs of him had been taken in

Stockholm, and now Hendil had to put these and a false name and address on an identity card.

The first few names Hendil suggested were impossible—because Pinnock could not pronounce them. An address was a worse problem. Finally both were found, and Pinnock's credentials were forged. He must pretend to be a deaf-mute, and although he probably thought this melodramatic, he agreed to do so. Before the war he had had business interests in Copenhagen, and in fact he spoke quite a bit of Danish.

At ten o'clock that night, after booking a hotel in Malmø for two nights hence, Pinnock was led to the harbour, and boarded a small grey boat. His crossing was cold but uneventful, and his boat docked next to the German fortress beside the dump at Amager. 'You'll have to be silent,' Hendil had cautioned, explaining that Pinnock would be taken right past a German sentry post.

Pinnock was met by four young Danes, members of a Resistance group known as '1944'. All four walked stiffly because they carried Sten guns under their coats. That night, carefully guarded, Pinnock slept in a flat in the same part of Copenhagen from which Niels Bohr had escaped.

Unknown to the Englishman or his guards, another group of Danes already had Pinnock under observation, and word of his presence was relayed to intelligence contacts outside Denmark within hours of his supposedly secret arrival.

In the morning, the Englishman and his four young friends bicycled right through the centre of Copenhagen, amid thousands of people silently but briskly cycling to work. One armed guard rode twenty yards ahead, and another twenty yards behind. If they encountered a German surprise road block, one of these Resistance men would create a disturbance to give Pinnock time to get away. The other group of Danes also followed the Englishman.

Remembering how to operate the back-pedal on his tall, black Danish bicycle, remembering to keep to the right,

Pinnock followed his escort out Strandvej, a main boulevard, to
Blidah Park, a group of modern four-storey flats in Hellerup.
There he would remain until he finished his work. Should he
have to flee, his friends told him, there were two other flats in
the neighbourhood where he could take refuge. Dozens of
Resistance men, well armed, were alert and on guard near by.
Food would be brought to Pinnock to avoid his having to
venture outside.

And so it was that, during the next day, the British Ministry
of Food had a branch office operating in German-occupied
Copenhagen. All Denmark's leading food experts visited
Blidah Park for talks with Pinnock, himself an expert in food
exports and imports. Had the problems he solved waited until
after the liberation, shipments of Danish foodstuffs vital to
Britain would have been delayed for months.

The morning Pinnock went to Blidah Park, a Danish intelligence man called at the British Embassy in Stockholm. Did
they know anything of a man who called himself Frank
Pinnock? Yes. Where was he? Skiing in northern Sweden, an
embassy secretary told the Dane.

An excited radio message reached London later in the day. It
stated that a German agent, passing himself as Frank Pinnock,
had entered Denmark on a Resistance boat. The man was
described, and the message asked if he should be liquidated.

Now Pinnock was in double jeopardy, for the second group
of Danes who had located him in Copenhagen were Resistance
intelligence men whose liaison with England did not include
contact with Ebbe Munck's Stockholm office. Luckily for
Pinnock, the intelligence message was seen by the Englishman's
colleagues in London. 'Good Lord!' one of them said,
'Pinnock's in Copenhagen!'

But this did not entirely satisfy military intelligence. What
if the Germans really had slipped an agent into the hands
of the Danish Resistance—an agent disguised as Frank
Pinnock?

Word was sent to the Resistance intelligence men in Copenhagen that, if the man who called himself Pinnock attempted
in any way to contact the Germans, he would be liquidated.

After he finished all of his business with the food exporters,
Pinnock's guards asked him what he wanted to do until it was
time for him to return to Sweden. Would it be all right if he
visited friends, Pinnock asked.

That night, in a private home in Copenhagen, a party was
given in the Englishman's honour, and after it, well guarded and
still followed by a group of liquidation men, Pinnock was
returned to Blidah Park for his last night's sleep in occupied
Copenhagen. Before he retired, he was told what escape route
he should follow if there was trouble during the night.

Pinnock slept soundly. In the morning his guards asked him
if he had been disturbed. No, he had not. 'Well,' one of the
young Danes said, 'we thought that you might at least have
heard the air-raid sirens. They kept us up all night.'

That evening, after dark, the four young Resistance men
took the Englishman back toward the Amager dump, and there
they waited at the foot of the German fortress. Pinnock's trip
to Sweden was speedy; the wind was behind his boat all the
way, and he arrived thirty-five minutes earlier than Hendil had
promised. Only after the war did Pinnock learn what would
have happened if he had, just for the fun of it, stopped to speak
to a German.

A week later, after making four unsuccessful orbits to try to
find the building, Embry's Mosquito bombers, again led by
Group Captain Bateson, hit the last of Denmark's Gestapo
headquarters, the one in the Odense agricultural college. The
building, which the Germans thought they had perfectly
hidden under camouflage nets, was demolished completely.

Information's post-war stand-by power station was now
ready. The British were moving up through south Schleswig,
and Jens Lillelund, still in London, knew he would never have

to parachute into Denmark. In Sweden, advance units of the Danish Brigade had been moved to the coast opposite Sealand. One of Leif Hendil's last shipping missions was to get a group of Allied correspondents to Amager where, on 4th May, they set foot on a corner of nominally-occupied Danish soil to file the sort of news stories that detail anticlimactic events. That same day one of the last Danish harbour pilots to quit his job, in Mariagerfjord, in North Jutland, was taken out and summarily executed by the Gestapo.

When British military units.were greeted in Copenhagen on 5th May by excited crowds, and by Ole Lippmann on behalf of the underground, German officers in Dagmarhus put down half-empty beer glasses to go out and surrender. Red, white, and blue arm-bands were everywhere. Traitors were rushed to the prisons, and patriots were released. German soldiers, un-certain what to do, dragged about the streets. Motor-cars and lorries labelled 'BOPA' and 'Holger Danske' cruised the streets. The little boats, now proudly flying the *Dannebrog*, deposited Resistance men in Denmark, and the *Røsnæs* arrived with the first units of the Danish Brigade.

The salvage tugs went to work to clear the harbours, and the lights were re-lit on the Sound buoys. The Freedom Council came out of hiding to take part in the first post-war Government. They re-enacted a death penalty, and the most vicious of the traitors were executed. Other collaborators received prison sentences.

It seemed a long time since Danes had thought of their country as 'Hitler's canary', but many of them wondered how much they had done in the war. Of four million Danes, 30,000 were members of organized Resistance groups, although had they stumbled into the right connections, doubtless thousands more would have joined. Three thousand Resistance men and women had been killed. Denmark was officially credited with helping to win Europe's freedom.

Four days after the city had been officially liberated, 40,000

German soldiers, many still armed, waited in Copenhagen. Only five hundred British troops were in the city, and VE day not withstanding, there could have been fighting that would have written a bloody finish to Denmark's war. The busy occupation forces had little time for sleep.

'Major Lund'—Ole Lippmann—reported to the British commander that there was a gun battle in progress between Danes and Germans outside a barracks in the centre of Copenhagen.

'Go down and stop it,' General Dewing, the British officer, ordered.

'Yes, sir,' Lippmann answered, saluting smartly.

As the Dane in the tight black civilian overcoat reached the door, Dewing called, 'Wait a minute, Major. Do you know what to do?'

'No, sir, but I'll try.'

Riding in an army lorry toward the barracks, Lippmann saw Danish Brigade soldiers sprawled in the street, sniping at the German camp. Several bullets hit his lorry.

Lippmann identified himself to the Danish commander. 'You must stop this shooting at once!'

'But, sir, those are *Germans* in there! They're shooting at us!'

Turning, Lippmann walked into the German camp and was saluted by the commander. 'The war is over,' Lippmann ordered. 'Tell your men to put down their guns.'

'But those Danes—'

'Yes, I know all about that,' Lippmann interrupted. 'As long as you stay in Copenhagen, there's going to be trouble. I'll give you two hours to get out of the city.'

'Where do we go, sir?" the German officer asked meekly.

'Start marching your men toward Korsør.' As the German saluted, Lippmann reminded him, 'Remember, two hours.'

Reporting back to General Dewing, Lippmann explained that he had personally told the Germans to quit Copenhagen.

'That's all very well, Major, but what happens to them when they get to Korsør?'

Lippmann, his face taut after several trying days, smiled. 'I don't know, sir. But at least we'll get a good night's sleep.'

FOREWORD

BY AIR CHIEF MARSHAL SIR BASIL EMBRY

G.C.B., K.B.B., D.S.O., D.F.C., A.F.C.

I COMMEND this book to those who prize the qualities of courage and patriotism and like to read about the deeds of brave people. It gives an excellent account of the work of the Underground Movement in Denmark during the Second World War, and recounts a story the telling of which has been long overdue.

I am glad it has been written because now it can be handed down to posterity and future generations will read with pride about the gallant work of the Danish Resistance during the long years of the German occupation of their homeland. Memories are short and now that the Danes no longer celebrate the liberation of their country, those who were unborn or not old enough to remember the German occupation might never realize what their forbears endured and fought for, so that they might enjoy the full fruits of freedom and live according to the Danish way of life.

I hope this book will be widely read in England and the United States because so little is known about the work of the Resistance Movements in Europe, yet they played an important role against the Axis Powers and made a major contribution to our ultimate victory.

Work in the Resistance called for cold blooded courage and a high code of honour. If caught in action or even suspected of working for the Resistance, prisoners would be subjected to the ordeal of prolonged interrogation by the Gestapo, accompanied by threats of violence and quite often terrible torture in an endeavour to make them give information about their comrades and the organization for which they worked. When this happened, as it often did, the easiest and longed for avenue of escape was death.

Just imagine working under such conditions—with the anxiety and fear of capture never far removed from their minds—and with the knowledge that their families and relations might be the subject of reprisal. Yet these people never wavered in their duty and carried on year after year—so that by the end of the war the Resistance Movement in Denmark had grown into a large organization and was a direct threat to the German forces of occupation.

One of my happiest memories of the war was my association with certain members of the Danish Resistance Movement and the small part I was able to take in their support.

AIR CHIEF MARSHAL SIR BASIL EMBRY
1957

Index